Vintage Style

Thirty knitting designs from ROWAN for men & women

Kaffe Fassett • Kim Hargreaves • Sarah Dallas • Martin Storey
Sharon Peake • Louisa Harding • Brandon Mably • Lucinda Guy

CONTENTS

Designers
Kaffe Fassett, Kim Hargreaves, Sarah Dallas,
Martin Storey, Sharon Peake, Louisa Harding,
Brandon Mably, Lucinda Guy

Photographer Joey Toller

Stylist Kim Hargreaves

Hair & Make-up Annabel Hobbs

Models Ivana Filipovic, Nina Hartley
& Charlie Gardner

Design Layout Simon Wagstaff

Freelance Journalist Alex Buxton

Internet: www.knitrowan.com
Email: vintagestyle@knitrowan.com

British library Cataloguing in
Publication Data
Rowan Yarns
Vintage Style
ISBN 1-904485-21-9

Copyright Rowan Yarns 2004
First published in Great Britain in 2004 by
Rowan Yarns Ltd, Green Lane Mill,
Holmfirth, West Yorkshire, HD9 2DX

INTRODUCTION

When we seek comfort and reassurance, we look not
to the future with all its uncertainties but to the past.
Half a century on, the post-war period of the late 40's,
50's and 60's seems a golden, unhurried age when
life was sweetly simple and when time passed with
a less hurried beat.

It's to this era, with its mood of renewal, that we look
for fashion inspiration. After the frugality of the war
years, women rejoiced in wearing swirling skirts, soft
knitwear and exuberant prints. Men, back home once
more and out of their stifling uniforms, relaxed in roll-
necked sweaters and corduroy trousers, rediscovering
the pleasures of colour.

We've drawn on old photographs, films (such as
Chocolat and Amelie) and archives of knitting patterns
to bring this period look alive. While being true to the
spirit of the age, we've updated and adapted classic
designs to make them easy to wear. In our photographs
we've created a look that exults in happy
combinations: old and new, floral and stripe, texture
and sleek.

Our title for the collection, Vintage Style, encapsulates
the feel for quality materials, for lasting craftsmanship,
for classic looks and above all for a real sense of style.
The knitwear you will find here won't date in the
passing of a season: it will improve with time and
become a treasure in its own right.

Alexandra Buxton

LAURENT
SHARON PEAKE

This little belted jacket, with its small collar, reflects the charm of a quiet French café with its lace curtains and shady interior. The decoration, intarsia flower motifs and embroidery, echoes antique textiles. The jacket works perfectly with a slim-line pleated skirt and delicate blouse. A perky hat completes the look.

LAURENT

SHARON PEAKE

YARN

	XS	S	M	L	XL	
To fit bust	81	86	91	97	102	cm
	32	34	36	38	40	in

Rowan Yorkshire Tweed DK and 4 ply, and Kid Classic

A DK Goose 352

	10	10	11	11	12	x 50gm

B KClass Crushed Velvet 825

	1	1	1	1	1	x 50gm

C DK Scarlet 344

	1	1	1	1	1	x 50gm

D KClass Juicy 827

	1	1	1	1	1	x 50gm

E 4ply Graze 286

	1	1	1	1	1	x 25gm

NEEDLES

1 pair 3¼ mm (no 10) (US 3) needles
1 pair 4mm (no 8) (US 6) needles

EXTRAS – 5 x 00321 buttons, and one 4 cm buckle 00365

TENSION

20 sts and 28 rows to 10 cm measured over stocking stitch using 4mm (US 6) needles.

BACK

Cast on 91 (95: 101: 105: 111) sts using 3¼ mm (US 3) needles and yarn A.
Rows 1 and 2: Knit.

Row 3 (RS): K1, *slip 1 st purlwise, K1, rep from * to end.
Row 4: K1, *slip 1 st purlwise with yarn at front (WS) of work, K1, rep from * to end.
Rows 5 and 6: Knit.
Row 7: K2, *slip 1 st purlwise, K1, rep from * to last st, K1.
Row 8: K2, *slip 1 st purlwise with yarn at front (WS) of work, K1, rep from * to last st, K1.
These 8 rows form border patt.
Cont in border patt for 8 cm, dec 1 st at end of last row and ending with a WS row.
90 (94: 100: 104: 110) sts.
Change to 4mm (US 6) needles.
Beg with a K row, work in st st for 2 rows, ending with a WS row.
Starting and ending rows as indicated and using the **intarsia** technique as described on the information page, cont in patt from chart for back, which is worked entirely in st st beg with a K row, as folls:
Dec 1 st at each end of 5th and foll 6th row.
86 (90: 96: 100: 106) sts.
Cont straight until chart row 16 has been completed, ending with a WS row.
Break off contrasts and cont in st st using yarn A only.
Dec 1 st at each end of next and foll 6th row.
82 (86: 92: 96: 102) sts.
Cont straight until back measures 22 (23: 23: 24: 24) cm, ending with a WS row.

Inc 1 st at each end of next and every foll 10th row until there are 90 (94: 100: 104: 110) sts.
Work 17 rows, ending with a WS row. (Back should measure 39 (40: 40: 41: 41) cm.)
Shape armholes
Cast off 4 (5: 5: 6: 6) sts at beg of next 2 rows.
82 (84: 90: 92: 98) sts.
Dec 1 st at each end of next 5 (5: 7: 7: 9) rows, then on foll 2 alt rows, then on foll 4th row.
66 (68: 70: 72: 74) sts.
Cont straight until armhole measures 20 (20: 21: 21: 22) cm, ending with a WS row.
Shape shoulders and back neck
Cast off 6 (6: 6: 6: 7) sts at beg of next 2 rows.
54 (56: 58: 60: 60) sts.
Next row (RS): Cast off 6 (6: 6: 6: 7) sts, K until there are 10 (10: 11: 11: 10) sts on right needle and turn, leaving rem sts on a holder.
Work each side of neck separately.
Cast off 4 sts at beg of next row.
Cast off rem 6 (6: 7: 7: 6) sts.
With RS facing, rejoin yarn to rem sts, cast off centre 22 (24: 24: 26: 26) sts, K to end.
Complete to match first side, reversing shapings.

LEFT FRONT

Cast on 51 (53: 57: 59: 61) sts using 3¼ mm (US 3) needles and yarn A.
Work in border patt as given for back for 8 cm, ending with a RS row.
Next row (WS): Patt 7 sts and slip these sts onto a holder, M1, patt to last 0 (0: 2: 2: 0) sts,

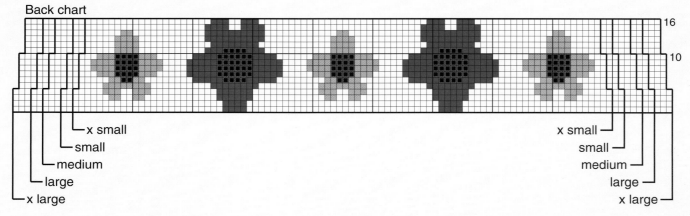

Back chart

16

10

x small
small
medium
large
x large

x small
small
medium
large
x large

(K2tog) 0 (0: 1: 1: 0) times.

45 (47: 50: 52: 55) sts.

Change to 4mm (US 6) needles.

Beg with a K row, work in st st for 4 rows, ending with a WS row.

Starting and ending rows as indicated, cont in patt from chart for lower left front as folls:

Dec 1 st at beg of 3rd and every foll 6th row until 42 (44: 47: 49: 52) sts rem.

Cont straight until chart row 18 has been completed, ending with a WS row.

Break off contrasts and cont in st st using yarn A only.

Dec 1 st at beg of 3rd row. 41 (43: 46: 48: 51) sts.

Cont straight until left front measures 22 (23: 23: 24: 24) cm, ending with a WS row.

Inc 1 st at beg of next and foll 10th row.

43 (45: 48: 50: 53) sts.

Work 7 rows, ending with a WS row.

Place Chart

Next row (RS): Using yarn A K17 (19: 22: 24: 27), work last 26 sts as row 1 of chart

for upper left front.

Next row: Work first 26 sts as row 2 of chart for upper left front, using yarn A P to end.

These 2 rows set position of chart with side edge sts in st st using yarn A.

Working rem 58 rows of chart and then completing work in st st using yarn A only, cont as folls:

Inc 1 st at beg of next and foll 10th row.

45 (47: 50: 52: 55) sts.

Work 5 rows, ending with a WS row.

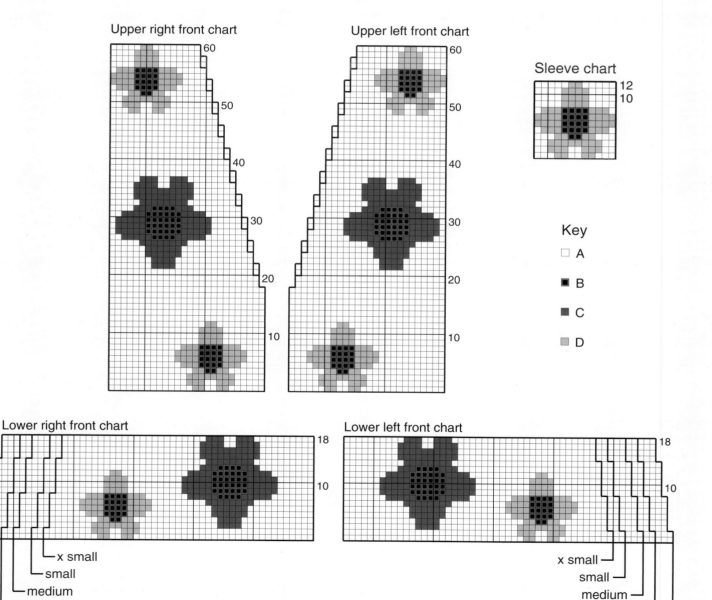

Shape front slope

Keeping patt correct, dec 1 st at end of next and foll 0 (0: 0: 1: 0) alt rows, then on every foll 4th row until 42 (44: 47: 48: 52) sts rem.
Work 3 (3: 3: 1: 3) rows, ending with a WS row. (Left front now matches back to beg of armhole shaping.)

Shape armhole

Keeping patt correct, cast off 4 (5: 5: 6: 6) sts at beg and dec 1 (1: 1: 0: 1) st at end of next row. 37 (38: 41: 42: 45) sts.
Work 1 row.
Dec 1 st at armhole edge of next 5 (5: 7: 7: 9) rows, then on foll 2 alt rows, then on foll 4th row and at same time dec 1 st at front slope edge on 3rd (3rd: 3rd: next: 3rd) and every foll 4th row. 26 (27: 27: 28: 29) sts.
Dec 1 st at front slope edge only on 2nd (2nd: 4th: 2nd: 2nd) and every foll 4th row to 20 (18: 20: 19: 21) sts, then on every foll 6th (-: 6th: -: 6th) row until 18 (-: 19: -: 20) sts rem.
Cont straight until left front matches back to start of shoulder shaping, ending with a WS row.

Shape shoulder

Cast off 6 (6: 6: 6: 7) sts at beg of next and foll alt row. Work 1 row.
Cast off rem 6 (6: 7: 7: 6) sts.

RIGHT FRONT

Cast on 51 (53: 57: 59: 61) sts using 3¼ mm (US 3) needles and yarn A.
Work in border patt as given for back for 8 cm, ending with a RS row.

Next row (WS): (K2tog) 0 (0: 1: 1: 0) times, patt to last 7 sts, M1 and turn, leaving rem 7 sts on a holder. 45 (47: 50: 52: 55) sts.
Change to 4mm (US 6) needles.
Beg with a K row, work in st st for 4 rows, ending with a WS row.
Starting and ending rows as indicated, cont in patt from chart for lower right front as folls:
Dec 1 st at end of 3rd and every foll 6th row until 42 (44: 47: 49: 52) sts rem.

Cont straight until chart row 18 has been completed, ending with a WS row.
Break off contrasts and cont in st st using yarn A only.
Dec 1 st at end of 3rd row.
41 (43: 46: 48: 51) sts.
Cont straight until right front measures 22 (23: 23: 24: 24) cm, ending with a WS row.
Inc 1 st at end of next and foll 10th row.
43 (45: 48: 50: 53) sts.

Place Chart

Work 7 rows, ending with a WS row.
Next row (RS): Work first 26 sts as row 1 of chart for upper right front, using yarn A K to end.
Next row: Using yarn A P17 (19: 22: 24: 27), work last 26 sts as row 2 of chart for upper right front.
These 2 rows set position of chart with side edge sts in st st using yarn A.
Working rem 58 rows of chart and then completing work in st st using yarn A only, complete to match left front, reversing shapings.

SLEEVES (both alike)

Cast on 53 (53: 55: 57: 57) sts using 3¼ mm (US 3) needles and yarn A.
Work in border patt as given for back, dec 1 st at each end of 9th and every foll 6th row until 47 (47: 49: 51: 51) sts rem.
Work a further 4 rows, dec 1 st at end of last row and ending with a RS row.
46 (46: 48: 50: 50) sts.
Place markers at both ends of last row.
Change to 4mm (US 6) needles.
Beg with a K row (to reverse RS of work), cont in st st, shaping sides by inc 1 st at each end of 9th (7th: 7th: 7th: 7th) and foll 10th (8th: 8th: 8th: 8th) row. 50 (50: 52: 54: 54) sts.

Place Chart

Work 3 (7: 7: 7: 7) rows, ending with a WS row.
Next row (RS): Using yarn A (inc in first st) 0 (1: 0: 0: 1) times, K19 (18: 20: 21: 20), work

next 12 sts as row 1 of chart for sleeve, using yarn A K to last 0 (1: 0: 0: 1) st, (inc in last st) 0 (1: 0: 0: 1) times.
50 (52: 52: 54: 56) sts.
Next row: Using yarn A 19 (20: 20: 21: 22), work next 12 sts as row 2 of chart for sleeve, using yarn A P to end.
These 2 rows set position of chart with sts either side in st st using yarn A.
Cont as set, inc 1 st at each end of 5th (9th: next: next: 7th) row.
52 (54: 54: 56: 58) sts.
Work a further 5 (1: 9: 9: 3) rows, completing chart row 12 and ending with a WS row.
Break off contrasts and cont using yarn A only.
Inc 1 st at each end of 5th (9th: next: next: 5th) and every foll 10th (10th: 10th: 10th: 8th) row to 62 (68: 70: 72: 64) sts, then on every foll 12th (-: -: -: 10th) row until there are 66 (-: -: -: 74) sts.
Cont straight until sleeve measures 42 (42: 43: 43: 43) cm from markers, ending with a WS row.

Shape top

Cast off 4 (5: 5: 6: 6) sts at beg of next 2 rows. 58 (58: 60: 60: 62) sts.
Dec 1 st at each end of next 5 rows, then on foll 2 alt rows, then on every foll 4th row until 36 (36: 38: 38: 40) sts rem.
Work 1 row, ending with a WS row.
Dec 1 st at each end of next and every foll alt row to 28 sts, then on foll 3 rows, ending with a WS row.
Cast off rem 22 sts.

MAKING UP

PRESS as described on the information page.
Join both shoulder seams using back stitch, or mattress stitch if preferred.

Button band and left collar

Slip 7 sts from left front holder onto 3¼ mm needles and rejoin yarn A with RS facing.
Cont in border patt until band, when slightly stretched, fits up left front opening edge to start of front slope shaping, ending with a WS row.
Inc 1 st at beg of next and every foll 4th row

until there are 28 sts, taking inc sts into patt.
Cont straight until this collar section,
unstretched, fits up left front slope and across
to centre back neck.
Cast off.
Mark positions for 5 buttons on this band –
first to come just above border patt, last to
come just below start of front slope shaping,
and rem 3 buttons evenly spaced between.

Buttonhole band and right collar
Slip 7 sts from right front holder onto 3$^{1}/_{4}$ mm
needles and rejoin yarn A with WS facing.
Work 1 row.

Next row (buttonhole row) (RS): Patt 2 sts,
work 2 tog, yrn, patt to end.
Working a further 4 buttonholes to correspond
with positions marked on left front for buttons,
complete to match button band and left collar,
reversing shapings.
Join centre back seam of collar sections, then
slip stitch bands and collar in place.

Embroidery
Using yarn E and diagram as a guide,
embroider chain stitch lines onto all pieces.
See information page for finishing instructions,
setting in sleeves using the set-in method
and reversing sleeve seam below markers
for turn-back.

Belt
Cast on 9 sts using 3$^{1}/_{4}$ mm (US 3) needles
and yarn A.
Work in border patt as given for back for
70 (75: 80: 85: 90) cm.
Cast off.
Attach buckle to one end of belt.

Chain Stitch

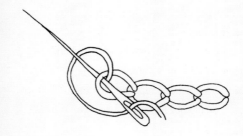

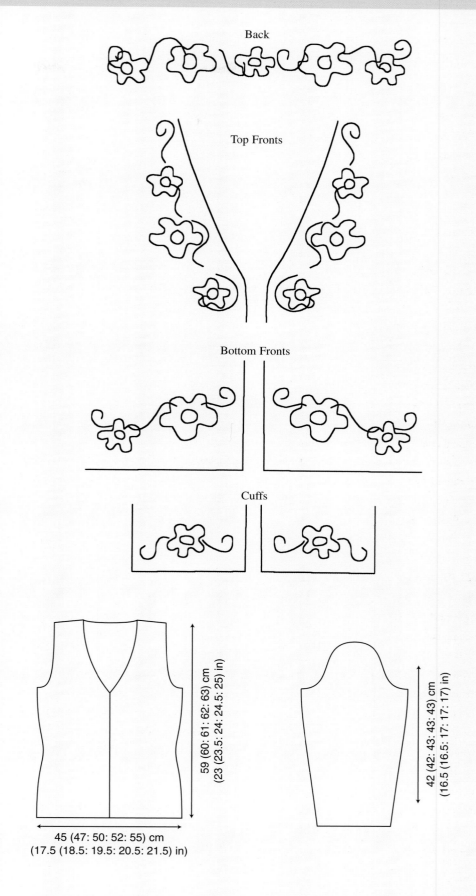

CHINESE BASKET
KAFFE FASSETT

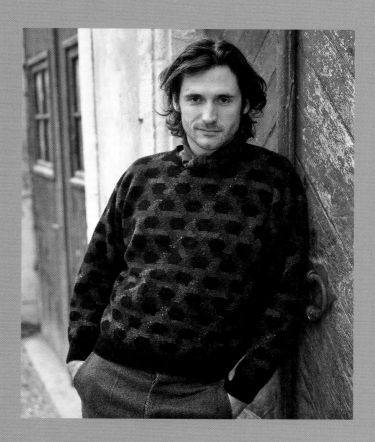

The criss-crossing of rich dark colours create a
masculine look in this geometric jumper.
Ruggedly handsome, it takes its colour and design
inspiration from nature: woods and farms, ploughed
fields and log piles, stacked up in preparation
for winter months ahead.

CHINESE BASKET
KAFFE FASSETT

YARN

	S	M	L	XL	XXL	
To fit chest	97	102	107	112	117	cm
	38	40	42	44	46	in

Rowan Yorkshire Tweed 4 ply

SWEATER

A Whiskers 283

9	9	9	10	10	x 25gm

B Lustre 282

3	3	3	3	3	x 25gm

C Explode 277

3	3	3	3	3	x 25gm

D Mulled Wine 279

5	5	6	6	6	x 25gm

E Knight 281

3	3	3	3	4	x 25gm

F Radiant 276

3	3	3	3	3	x 25gm

G Bristle 278

2	2	2	3	3	x 25gm

SLIPOVER

A Whiskers 283

4	4	5	5	5	x 25gm

B Lustre 282

2	2	2	2	2	x 25gm

C Explode 277

2	2	2	2	2	x 25gm

D Mulled Wine 279

2	2	2	2	2	x 25gm

E Knight 281

2	2	2	2	2	x 25gm

F Radiant 276

2	2	2	2	2	x 25gm

G Bristle 278

2	2	2	2	2	x 25gm

NEEDLES

1 pair 2¼ mm (no 13) (US 1) needles
1 pair 3mm (no 11) (US 2/3) needles

TENSION

28 sts and 40 rows to 10 cm measured over patterned stocking stitch using 3mm (US 2/3) needles.

SWEATER

BACK

Cast on 157 (163: 171: 177: 185) sts using 2¼ mm (US 1) needles and yarn E.

Break off yarn E and join in yarn A.

Row 1 (RS): K1, *P1, K1, rep from * to end.

Row 2: P1, *K1, P1, rep from * to end.

These 2 rows form rib.

Cont in rib for 6 cm, inc 1 st at end of last row and ending with a WS row.

158 (164: 172: 178: 186) sts.

Change to 3mm (US 2/3) needles.

Starting and ending rows as indicated, using the **intarsia** technique as described on the information page and repeating the 108 row patt repeat throughout, cont in patt from chart, which is worked entirely in st st beg with a K row, as folls:

Cont straight until back measures 35 (35: 36: 36: 37) cm, ending with a WS row.

Shape armholes

Keeping patt correct, cast off 7 sts at beg of next 2 rows. 144 (150: 158: 164: 172) sts.

Dec 1 st at each end of next 5 rows.

134 (140: 148: 154: 162) sts.

Cont straight until armhole measures 25 (26: 26: 27: 27) cm, ending with a WS row.

Shape shoulders and back neck

Cast off 13 (14: 15: 16: 17) sts at beg of next 2 rows.

108 (112: 118: 122: 128) sts.

Next row (RS): Cast off 13 (14: 15: 16: 17) sts, patt until there are 18 (18: 20: 20: 21) sts on right needle and turn, leaving rem sts on a holder.

Work each side of neck separately.

Cast off 4 sts at beg of next row.

Cast off rem 14 (14: 16: 16: 17) sts.

With RS facing, rejoin yarns to rem sts, cast off centre 46 (48: 48: 50: 52) sts, patt to end.

Complete to match first side, reversing shapings.

FRONT

Work as given for back until 24 (24: 26: 26: 26) rows less have been worked than on back to start of shoulder shaping, end with a WS row.

Shape neck

Next row (RS): Patt 57 (59: 64: 66: 69) sts and turn, leaving rem sts on a holder.

Work each side of neck separately.

Cast off 4 sts at beg of next and foll alt row.

49 (51: 56: 58: 61) sts.

Dec 1 st at neck edge of next 5 rows, then on foll 2 (2: 3: 3: 3) alt rows, then on every foll 4th row until 40 (42: 46: 48: 51) sts rem.

Work 3 rows, ending with a WS row.

Shape shoulder

Cast off 13 (14: 15: 16: 17) sts at beg of next and foll alt row.

Work 1 row.

Cast off rem 14 (14: 16: 16: 17) sts.

With RS facing, rejoin yarns to rem sts, cast off centre 20 (22: 20: 22: 24) sts, patt to end.

Complete to match first side, reversing shapings.

SLEEVES (both alike)

Cast on 79 (79: 81: 83: 83) sts using 2¼ mm (US 1) needles and yarn E.

Break off yarn E and join in yarn A.

Work in rib as given for back for 6 cm, inc 1 st at end of last row and ending with a WS row.

80 (80: 82: 84: 84) sts.

Change to 3mm (US 2/3) needles.

Starting and ending rows as indicated, cont in patt from chart, shaping sides by inc 1 st at each end of 5th and every foll 6th row to 104 (96: 102: 100: 100) sts, then on every foll 4th row until there are 140 (146: 146: 152: 152) sts, taking inc sts into patt.

Cont straight until sleeve measures 48 (49: 49: 50: 50) cm, ending with a WS row.

Shape top

Keeping patt correct, cast off 7 sts at beg of next 2 rows.

126 (132: 132: 138: 138) sts.

Dec 1 st at each end of next and foll 6 alt rows.
Work 1 row, ending with a WS row.
Cast off rem 112 (118: 118: 124: 124) sts.

MAKING UP

PRESS as described on the information page.
Join right shoulder seam using back stitch, or
mattress stitch if preferred.

Neckband

With RS facing, using 2¹/₄ mm (US 1) needles
and yarn A, pick up and knit 30 (30: 32:
32: 32) sts down left side of neck, 19 (21: 19:
21: 23) sts from front, 30 (30: 32: 32: 32) sts
up right side of neck, then 54 (56: 56: 58: 60) sts
from back. 133 (137: 139: 143: 147) sts.
Work in rib as given for back for 9 rows.
Break off yarn A and join in yarn E.
Work 1 row.
Cast off in rib (on WS).
See information page for finishing instructions,
setting in sleeves using the shallow set-in method.

SLIPOVER

BACK

Cast on 145 (151: 159: 165: 173) sts using
2¹/₄ mm (US 1) needles and yarn E.
Break off yarn E and join in yarn A.
Row 1 (RS): K1, *P1, K1, rep from * to end.
Row 2: P1, *K1, P1, rep from * to end.
These 2 rows form rib.
Cont in rib for 6 cm, inc 1 st at end of last row
and ending with a WS row.
146 (152: 160: 166: 174) sts.
Change to 3mm (US 2/3) needles.
Starting and ending rows as indicated, using
the intarsia technique as described on the
information page and repeating the 108 row
patt repeat throughout, cont in patt from chart,
which is worked entirely in st st beg with a K
row, as folls:
Cont straight until back measures 35 (35: 36:
36: 37) cm, ending with a WS row.

Shape armholes

Keeping patt correct, cast off 6 (7: 7: 8: 8) sts
at beg of next 2 rows.
134 (138: 146: 150: 158) sts.**
Dec 1 st at each end of next 7 (7: 9: 9: 11)
rows, then on foll 4 (5: 5: 6: 6) alt rows, then
on every foll 4th row until 108 (110: 114:
116: 120) sts rem.
Cont straight until armhole measures 25 (26:
26: 27: 27) cm, ending with a WS row.

Shape shoulders and back neck

Cast off 10 (10: 11: 11: 11) sts at beg of
next 2 rows. 88 (90: 92: 94: 98) sts.
Next row (RS): Cast off 10 (10: 11: 11: 11)
sts, patt until there are 14 (14: 14: 14: 15) sts
on right needle and turn, leaving rem sts
on a holder.
Work each side of neck separately.
Cast off 4 sts at beg of next row.
Cast off rem 10 (10: 10: 10: 11) sts.
With RS facing, rejoin yarns to rem sts, cast off
centre 40 (42: 42: 44: 46) sts, patt to end.
Complete to match first side, reversing shapings.

FRONT

Work as given for back to **.
Dec 1 st at each end of next 6 rows, ending
with a WS row.
122 (126: 134: 138: 146) sts.

Divide for neck

Next row (RS): K2tog, patt 57 (59: 63:
65: 69) sts, K2tog and turn, leaving rem sts
on a holder.
Work each side of neck separately.
Dec 0 (0: 1: 1: 1) st at armhole edge of next row.
59 (61: 64: 66: 70) sts.
Dec 1 st at armhole edge of next 1 (1: 1: 1: 3)
rows, then on foll 3 (4: 5: 6: 6) alt rows, then
on 2 foll 4th rows and at same time dec 1 st at
neck edge on next and every foll alt row.
45 (45: 46: 46: 47) sts.
Dec 1 st at neck edge only on 2nd (2nd: 2nd:
4th: 2nd) and foll 2 (1: 0: 0: 0) alt rows, then

on every foll 4th row to 35 (35: 37: 37: 38) sts,
then on every foll 6th row until 30 (30: 32:
32: 33) sts rem.
Cont straight until front matches back to start
of shoulder shaping, ending with a WS row.

Shape shoulder

Cast off 10 (10: 11: 11: 11) sts at beg of next
and foll alt row.
Work 1 row.
Cast off rem 10 (10: 10: 10: 11) sts.
With RS facing, rejoin yarns to rem sts, K2tog,
patt to last 2 sts, K2tog.
Complete to match first side, reversing shapings.

MAKING UP

PRESS as described on the information page.
Join right shoulder seam using back stitch, or
mattress stitch if preferred.

Neckband

With RS facing, using 2¹/₄ mm (US 1) needles
and yarn A, pick up and knit 78 (80: 80:
84: 84) sts down left side of neck, one st from
base of V (mark this st with a coloured thread),
78 (80: 80: 84: 84) sts up right side of neck,
then 48 (50: 50: 52: 54) sts from back.
205 (211: 211: 221: 223) sts.
Row 1 (WS): P1, *K1, P1, rep from * to end.
This row sets position of rib.
Keeping rib correct, cont as folls:
Row 2: Rib to within 2 sts of marked st, K2tog
tbl, K marked st, K2tog, rib to end.
Row 3: Rib to marked st, P marked st, rib
to end.
Rep last 2 rows 3 times more.
197 (203: 203: 213: 215) sts.
Break off yarn A and join in yarn E.
Row 10: As row 2.
Cast off in rib (on WS).
Join left shoulder and neckband seam.

Armhole borders (both alike)

With RS facing, using 2¹/₄ mm (US 1) needles
and yarn A, pick up and knit 159 (167: 167:
175: 175) sts around armhole edge.

108 row patt repeat

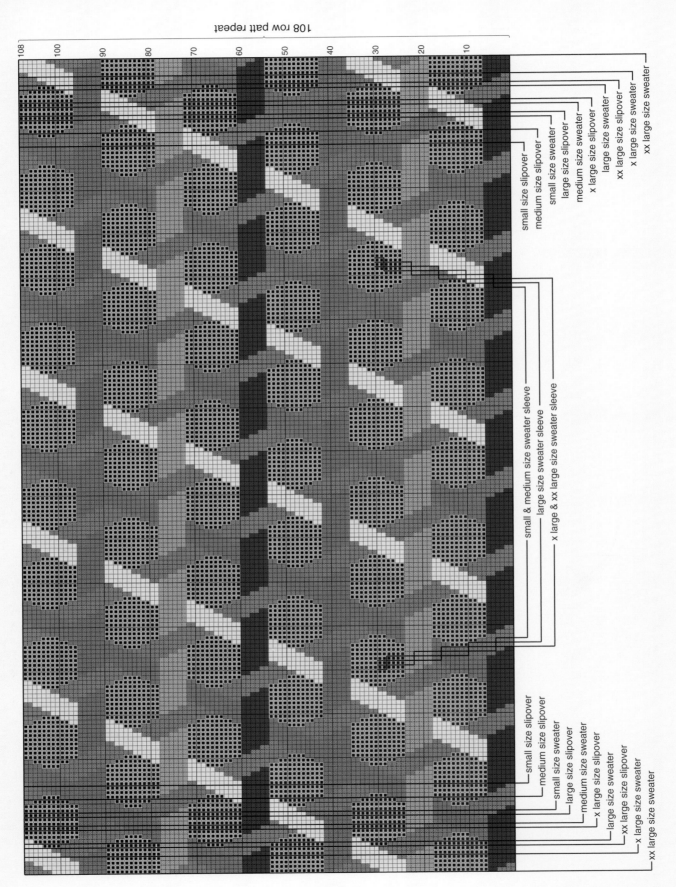

108 100 90 80 70 60 50 40 30 20 10

small size slipover
medium size slipover
small size sweater
large size slipover
medium size sweater
x large size slipover
large size sweater
xx large size slipover
x large size sweater
xx large size sweater

small & medium size sweater sleeve
large size sweater sleeve
x large & xx large size sweater sleeve

small size slipover
medium size slipover
small size sweater
large size slipover
medium size sweater
x large size slipover
large size sweater
xx large size slipover
x large size sweater
xx large size sweater

Work in rib as given for back for 7 rows.

Break off yarn A and join in yarn E.

Work 1 row.

Cast off in rib (on WS).

See information page for finishing instructions.

SWEATER

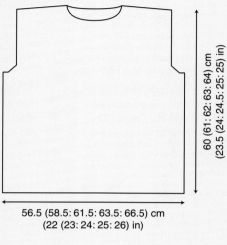

60 (61: 62: 63: 64) cm
(23.5 (24: 24.5: 25: 25) in)

56.5 (58.5: 61.5: 63.5: 66.5) cm
(22 (23: 24: 25: 26) in)

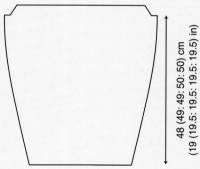

48 (49: 49: 50: 50) cm
(19 (19.5: 19.5: 19.5: 19.5) in)

SLIPOVER

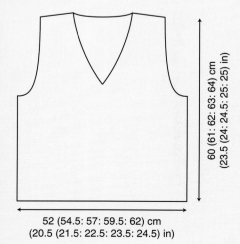

60 (61: 62: 63: 64) cm
(23.5 (24: 24.5: 25: 25) in)

52 (54.5: 57: 59.5: 62) cm
(20.5 (21.5: 22.5: 23.5: 24.5) in)

SUZETTE

KIM HARGREAVES

This striped cardigan has a disarming innocence, knitted up in blues, browns and naturals, and worn here with an open-necked blouse. The stripes are interspersed with rows of folkloric motifs, inspired by craft knitwear. It's a gentle look redolent of weekends in the country, precious time away from the hustle-bustle of the city.

SUZETTE

KIM HARGREAVES

YARN

	XS	S	M	L	XL	
To fit bust	81	86	91	97	102	cm
	32	34	36	38	40	in

Rowan Yorkshire Tweed 4 ply

		XS	S	M	L	XL	
A	Stainless 270	4	4	5	5	5	x 25gm
B	Radiant 276	2	2	2	2	2	x 25gm
C	Foxy 275	1	1	1	1	1	x 25gm
D	Butterscotch 272	1	1	1	1	2	x 25gm
E	Explode 277	2	2	2	2	2	x 25gm
F	Blessed 269	2	2	2	2	2	x 25gm
G	Highlander 266	2	2	2	2	2	x 25gm
H	Sheer 267	2	2	2	2	2	x 25gm
J	Enchant 268	2	2	2	2	2	x 25gm

NEEDLES

1 pair 3^1/$_4$ mm (no 10) (US 3) needles

CROCHET HOOK

3.25mm (no 10) (US D3) crochet hook

BUTTONS – 9 x 00315

TENSION

30 sts and 37 rows to 10 cm measured over patterned stocking stitch using 3^1/$_4$ mm (US 3) needles.

CROCHET ABBREVIATIONS

dc = double crochet; **ch** = chain; **ss** = slip stitch.

BACK

Cast on 119 (127: 135: 143: 151) sts using 3^1/$_4$ mm (US 3) needles and yarn A.

Starting and ending rows as indicated and using the **fairisle** technique as described on the information page, cont in patt from chart for body, which is worked entirely in st st beg with a K row, as folls:

Dec 1 st at each end of 23rd (25th: 25th: 27th: 27th) and every foll 6th row until 107 (115: 123: 131: 139) sts rem.

Work 15 (17: 17: 19: 19) rows, ending with a WS row.

Inc 1 st at each end of next and every foll 8th row to 119 (127: 135: 143: 151) sts, then on every foll 6th row until there are 125 (133: 141: 149: 157) sts, taking inc sts into patt.

Cont straight until chart row 136 (140: 140: 144: 144) has been completed, ending with a WS row. (Back should measure 37 (38: 38: 39: 39) cm.)

Shape armholes

Keeping patt correct, cast off 4 (5: 5: 6: 6) sts at beg of next 2 rows. 117 (123: 131: 137: 145) sts.

Dec 1 st at each end of next 7 (7: 9: 9: 11) rows, then on foll 4 (5: 5: 6: 6) alt rows. 95 (99: 103: 107: 111) sts.

Cont straight until chart row 214 (218: 222: 226: 230) has been completed, ending with a WS row. (Armhole should measure 21 (21: 22: 22: 23) cm.)

Shape shoulders and back neck

Cast off 8 (9: 9: 10: 10) sts at beg of next 2 rows. 79 (81: 85: 87: 91) sts.

Next row (RS): Cast off 8 (9: 9: 10: 10) sts, patt until there are 13 (12: 14: 13: 15) sts on right needle and turn, leaving rem sts on a holder. Work each side of neck separately.

Cast off 4 sts at beg of next row.

Cast off rem 9 (8: 10: 9: 11) sts.

With RS facing, rejoin yarns to rem sts, cast off centre 37 (39: 39: 41: 41) sts, patt to end. Complete to match first side, reversing shapings.

LEFT FRONT

Cast on 60 (64: 68: 72: 76) sts using 3^1/$_4$ mm (US 3) needles and yarn A.

Starting and ending rows as indicated, cont in patt from chart for body as folls:

Dec 1 st at beg of 23rd (25th: 25th: 27th: 27th) and every foll 6th row until 54 (58: 62: 66: 70) sts rem.

Work 15 (17: 17: 19: 19) rows, ending with a WS row.

Inc 1 st at beg of next and every foll 8th row to 60 (64: 68: 72: 76) sts, then on every foll 6th row until there are 63 (67: 71: 75: 79) sts, taking inc sts into patt.

Cont straight until left front matches back to beg of armhole shaping, ending with a WS row.

Shape armhole

Keeping patt correct, cast off 4 (5: 5: 6: 6) sts at beg of next row.

59 (62: 66: 69: 73) sts.

Work 1 row.

Dec 1 st at each end of next 7 (7: 9: 9: 11) rows, then on foll 3 (3: 2: 2: 1) alt rows.

49 (52: 55: 58: 61) sts.

Work 1 row, ending with a WS row.

Shape front slope

Keeping patt correct, dec 1 st at each end of next and foll 0 (1: 2: 3: 4) alt rows.

47 (48: 49: 50: 51) sts.

Dec 1 st at front slope edge only on 2nd and foll 17 (18: 15: 16: 13) alt rows, then on every foll 4th row until 25 (26: 28: 29: 31) sts rem.

Cont straight until left front matches back to start of shoulder shaping, ending with a WS row.

Shape shoulder

Cast off 8 (9: 9: 10: 10) sts at beg of next and foll alt row.

Work 1 row.

Cast off rem 9 (8: 10: 9: 11) sts.

RIGHT FRONT

Work to match left front, reversing shapings.

SLEEVES (both alike)

Cast on 77 (77: 79: 81: 81) sts using 3^1/$_4$ mm (US 3) needles and yarn A.

Starting and ending rows as indicated and beg
with chart row 1 (5: 1: 5: 5), cont in patt from
chart for sleeve as folls:

Inc 1 st at each end of 15th row, taking inc sts
into patt. 79 (79: 81: 83: 83) sts.

Work a further 11 (7: 11: 7: 7) rows, ending
with chart row 26 and a WS row.

Starting and ending rows as indicated, cont in
patt from chart for body as folls:

Inc 1 st at each end of 5th (7th: 3rd: 7th: 5th)
and every foll 16th (14th: 12th: 12th: 12th) row
to 83 (89: 103: 105: 87) sts, then on every foll
14th (12th: -: -: 10th) row until there are
97 (99: -: -: 109) sts, taking inc sts into patt.

Cont straight until chart row 136 (140: 140:
144: 144) has been completed, ending with a
WS row. (Sleeve should measure 45 (45: 46:
46: 46) cm.)

Shape top

Keeping patt correct, cast off 4 (5: 5: 6: 6) sts at
beg of next 2 rows. 89 (89: 93: 93: 97) sts.

Dec 1 st at each end of next 3 rows, then on foll
2 alt rows, then on every foll 4th row until 59
(59: 63: 63: 67) sts rem.

Work 1 row, ending with a WS row.

Dec 1 st at each end of next and every foll alt
row to 55 sts, then on foll 7 rows, ending with a
WS row.

Cast off rem 41 sts.

MAKING UP

PRESS as described on the information page.
Join both shoulder seams using back stitch, or
mattress stitch if preferred.

See information page for finishing instructions,
setting in sleeves using the set-in method. Mark
positions for 9 buttonholes along right front opening
edge – first buttonhole 1 cm up from cast-on edge,
last buttonhole just below start of front slope shaping,
and rem 7 buttonholes evenly spaced between.

Edging

Using 3.25mm (US D3) crochet hook and yarn
A, attach yarn to base of right side seam and
work 1 round of dc evenly around entire hem,
front opening and neck edges, working 2 dc
into corners, ensuring edging lays flat and
ending with ss to first dc.

Break off yarn A and join in yarn C.

Next round: 1 ch (does NOT count as st), 1 dc
into each dc to end, working extra dc at corners
and missing dc as required along slopes to
ensure edging lays flat, ss to first dc.

Break off yarn C and join in yarn E.

Rep last round once more, making buttonholes
at positions marked by replacing (1 dc into
each of next 2 dc) with (2 ch, miss 2 dc).

Fasten off.

In same way, work edging around cast-on edge
of sleeves.

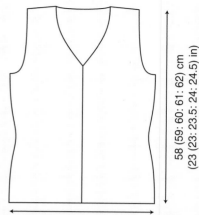

58 (59: 60: 61: 62) cm
(23: 23: 23.5: 24: 24.5) in)

41.5 (44.5: 47: 49.5: 52.5) cm
(16.5 (17.5: 18.5: 19.5: 20.5) in)

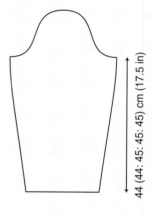

44 (44: 45: 45: 45) cm (17.5 in)

Key

A   F

B   G

C   H

D   J

E

Sleeve chart

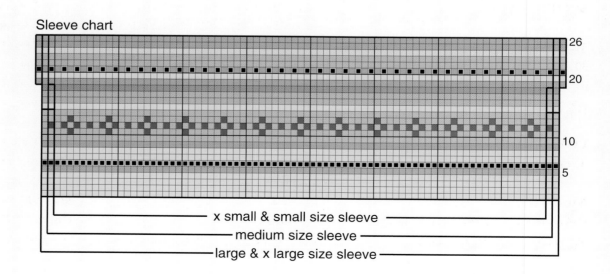

26
20
10
5

x small & small size sleeve
medium size sleeve
large & x large size sleeve

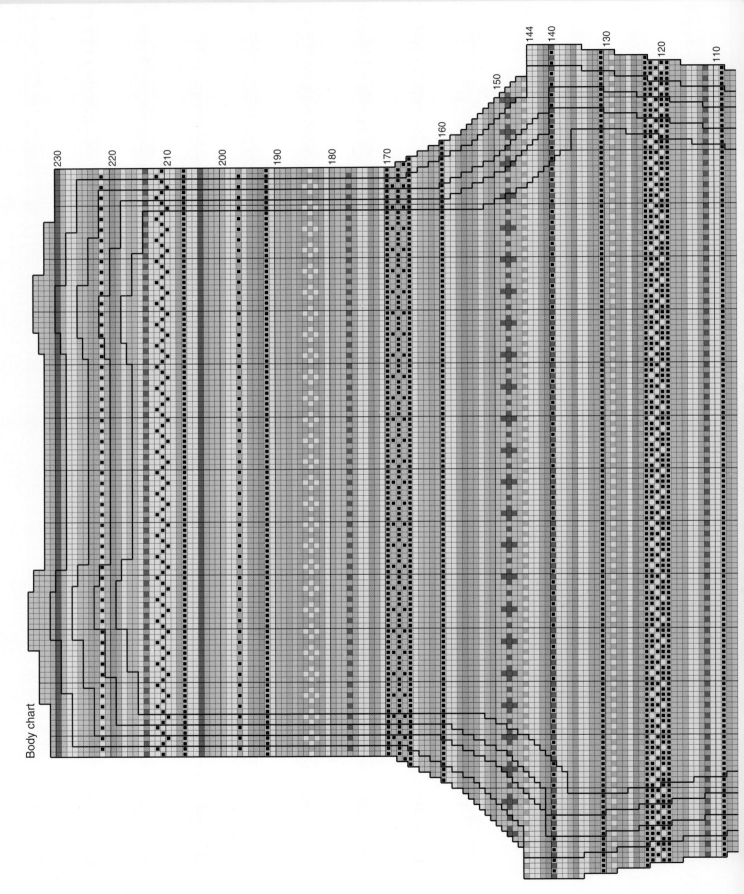

Body chart

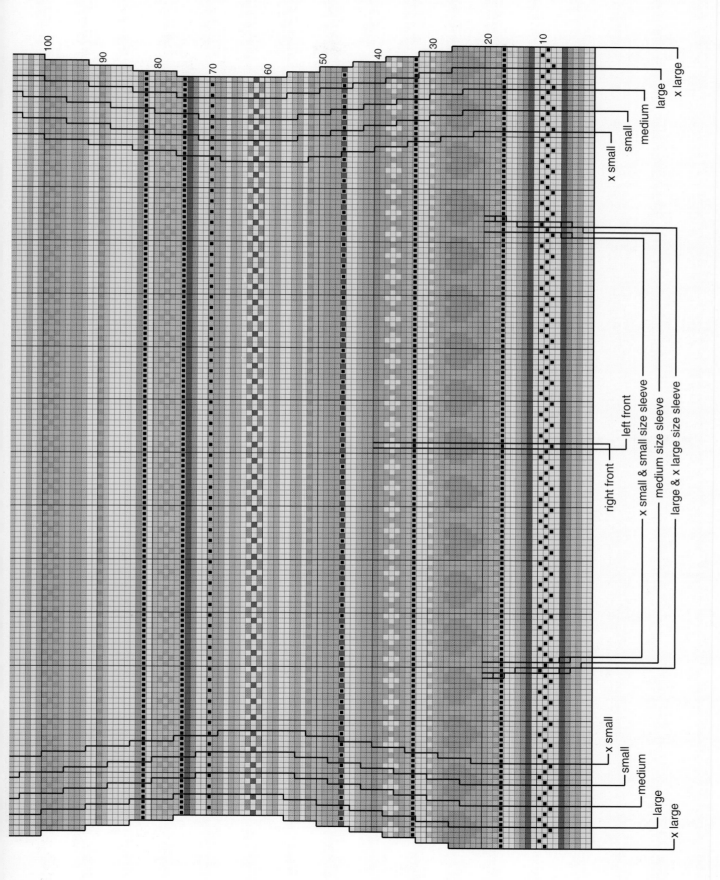

FLEUR
KIM HARGREAVES

Elegant and feminine, this cardigan is a real gem. The beautiful beaded detail around the edging and cuffs emphasises the simple, curving shape. The attention to detail takes us back to an artisan era, before the advent of mass-production, when garments were chosen with the greatest care and stored in tissue paper.

FLEUR

KIM HARGREAVES

YARN

	XS	S	M	L	XL	
To fit bust	81	86	91	97	102	cm
	32	34	36	38	40	in

Rowan 4 ply Soft

	6	7	7	8	8	x 50gm

(photographed in Leafy 367)

NEEDLES

1 pair 2³/₄ mm (no 12) (US 2) needles
1 pair 3¹/₄ mm (no 10) (US 3) needles

FASTENERS – 1 hook and eye

BEADS – approx 800 x 01020 beads

TENSION

28 sts and 36 rows to 10 cm measured over
stocking stitch using 3¹/₄ mm (US 3) needles.

SPECIAL ABBREVIATIONS

Bead 1 = place a bead by bringing yarn to front
(RS) of work and slipping bead up next to st
just worked, slip next st purlwise from left
needle to right needle and take yarn back to
back (WS) of work, leaving bead sitting in
front of slipped st on RS.

Beading note: Before starting to knit, thread
beads onto yarn. To do this, thread a fine
sewing needle (one that will easily pass through
the beads) with sewing thread. Knot ends of
thread and then pass end of yarn through this
loop. Thread a bead onto sewing thread and
then gently slide it along and onto knitting
yarn. Continue in this way until required
number of beads are on yarn.

BACK

Cast on 102 (108: 116: 122: 130) sts using
3¹/₄ mm (US 3) needles.
Beg with a K row, work in st st for 10 rows,
ending with a WS row.

Inc 1 st at each end of next and foll 10th row,
then on foll 8th row, then on foll 6th row, then
on every foll 4th row until there are 116 (122:
130: 136: 144) sts.
Work 1 row, ending with a WS row.
Inc 1 st at each end of next and foll 5 alt rows,
then on foll 5 rows, ending with a WS row.
138 (144: 152: 158: 166) sts.
Cast on 3 sts at beg of next 6 rows, 4 sts at beg
of foll 12 rows, 6 sts at beg of next 2 rows, 8
sts at beg of foll 4 rows, 10 sts at beg of next 2
rows, 18 sts at beg of foll 2 rows, and then
18 (18: 21: 21: 21) sts at beg of next 2 rows.
340 (346: 360: 366: 374) sts.
Cont straight until back measures 12 (12: 13:
13: 13) cm from last set of cast-on sts, ending
with a WS row.

Shape overarm seam and shoulders
Cast off 20 (22: 23: 25: 25) sts at beg of next 2
rows, 20 (20: 23: 23: 25) sts at beg of foll 4 rows,
20 sts at beg of next 4 rows, 18 sts at beg of foll 2
rows, and then 12 sts at beg of next 2 rows.
80 (82: 82: 84: 84) sts.

Shape back neck
Next row (RS): Cast off 10 sts, K until there
are 14 sts on right needle and turn, leaving rem
sts on a holder.
Work each side of neck separately.
Cast off 4 sts at beg of next row.
Cast off rem 10 sts.
With RS facing, rejoin yarn to rem sts, cast off
centre 32 (34: 34: 36: 36) sts, K to end.
Complete to match first side, reversing
shapings.

LEFT FRONT
Cast on 13 (16: 20: 23: 27) sts using 3¹/₄ mm
(US 3) needles.
Beg with a K row, work in st st as folls:
Work 1 row, ending with a RS row.
Cast on 4 sts at beg of next and foll alt row.
21 (24: 28: 31: 35) sts.
Work 1 row, ending with a RS row.

Inc 1 st at beg of next row and at same edge
(front opening edge) of next 4 rows, ending
with a WS row.
26 (29: 33: 36: 40) sts.
Inc 1 st at side seam edge of next and foll 10th
row, then on foll 8th row, then on foll 6th row
and at same time inc 1 st at front opening
edge of next 5 rows, then on foll 7 alt rows,
then on foll 4th row.
43 (46: 50: 53: 57) sts.
Inc 1 st at side seam edge of 4th and 2 foll 4th
rows **and at same time** inc 1 st at front
opening edge of 2nd and foll 6th row.
48 (51: 55: 58: 62) sts.
Work 1 row, ending with a WS row.
Inc 1 st at side seam edge of next and foll 5 alt
rows, then on foll 5 rows **and at same time** inc
1 st at front opening edge on next and foll 8th
row, ending with a WS row.
61 (64: 68: 71: 75) sts.
Cast on 3 sts at beg and inc 1 st at end of next row.
65 (68: 72: 75: 79) sts.
Work 1 row, ending with a WS row.
Cast on 3 sts at beg of next and foll alt row, 4
sts at beg of foll 6 alt rows, 6 sts at beg of foll
alt row, 8 sts at beg of foll 2 alt rows, 10 sts at
beg of foll alt row, 18 sts at beg of foll alt row,
and then 18 (18: 21: 21: 21) sts at beg of foll
alt row.
163 (166: 173: 176: 180) sts.
Cont straight until 7 (7: 7: 9: 9) rows less have
been worked than on back to start of overarm
and shoulder shaping, ending with a RS row.
Shape neck
Cast off 3 (4: 4: 4: 4) sts at beg of next row.
160 (162: 169: 172: 176) sts.
Dec 1 st at neck edge of next 6 rows, then on foll
0 (0: 0: 1: 1) alt row, ending with a WS row.
154 (156: 163: 165: 169) sts.
Shape overarm seam and shoulder
Cast off 20 (22: 23: 25: 25) sts at beg of next
row, 20 (20: 23: 23: 25) sts at beg of foll 2 alt
rows, 20 sts at beg of foll 2 alt rows, then 18 sts

at beg of foll alt row **and at same time** dec 1 st at neck edge of 2nd and foll 2 alt rows, then on foll 4th row. 32 sts.

Work 1 row, ending with a WS row.

Cast off 12 sts at beg of next row, then 10 sts at beg of foll alt row.

Work 1 row.

Cast off rem 10 sts.

RIGHT FRONT

Cast on 13 (16: 20: 23: 27) sts using $3^1/4$ mm (US 3) needles.

Beg with a K row, work in st st as folls:

Work 2 rows, ending with a WS row.

Cast on 4 sts at beg of next and foll alt row, ending with a RS row. 21 (24: 28: 31: 35) sts.

Inc 1 st at end of next row and at same edge (front opening edge) of next 4 rows, ending with a WS row. 26 (29: 33: 36: 40) sts.

Inc 1 st at side seam edge of next and foll 10th row, then on foll 8th row, then on foll 6th row **and at same time** inc 1 st at front opening edge of next 5 rows, then on foll 7 alt rows, then on foll 4th row. 43 (46: 50: 53: 57) sts.

Complete to match left front, reversing shapings.

MAKING UP

PRESS as described on the information page.

Join both overarm and shoulder seams using back stitch, or mattress stitch if preferred.

Cuffs (both alike)

With RS facing and using $2^3/4$ mm (US 2) needles, pick up and knit 65 (65: 69: 69: 69) sts across row-end edge of sleeve sections.

Row 1 (WS): P1, *K1, P1, rep from * to end.

Row 2: K1, *bead 1, K1, rep from * to end.

Row 3: As row 1.

Row 4: K1, *P1, K1, rep from * to end.

Rep last 4 rows once more.

Cast off in rib.

Join side, underarm and cuff seams using back stitch, or mattress stitch if preferred.

Left front edging

Cast on 9 sts using $2^3/4$ mm (US 2) needles.

Row 1 (RS): K2, *P1, K1, rep from * to last st, K1.

Row 2: K1, *P1, K1, rep from * to end.

Row 3: K2, *bead 1, K1, rep from * to last st, K1.

Row 4: As row 2.

These 4 rows form beaded rib patt.

Cont in beaded rib patt until edging fits neatly along left front opening edge, from left side seam to neck shaping, ending after patt row 4 and with a WS row.

Break yarn and leave sts on a holder.

Slip st edging in place.

Back and right front edging

Cast on 9 sts using $2^3/4$ mm (US 2) needles.

Work in beaded rib patt as given for left front edging until edging fits neatly across back cast-on edge and up right front opening edge, from right side seam to neck shaping, ending after patt row 4 and with a WS row.

Do NOT break yarn.

Slip st edging in place.

Neckband

With RS facing and using $2^3/4$ mm (US 2) needles, patt across 9 sts of back and right front edging, pick up and knit 26 (27: 27: 29: 29) sts up right side of neck, 41 (43: 43: 45: 45) sts from back, and 26 (27: 27: 29: 29) sts down left side of neck, then patt across 9 sts of left front edging. 111 (115: 115: 121: 121) sts.

Work in beaded rib patt as set by edging sts for 7 rows, ending with a WS row.

Cast off in rib.

Attach hook and eye at neck edge.

121.5 (123.5: 128.5: 131: 133.5) cm (48 (48.5: 50.5: 51.5: 52.5) in)

42 (42: 43: 43: 43) cm (16.5 (16.5: 17: 17: 17) in)

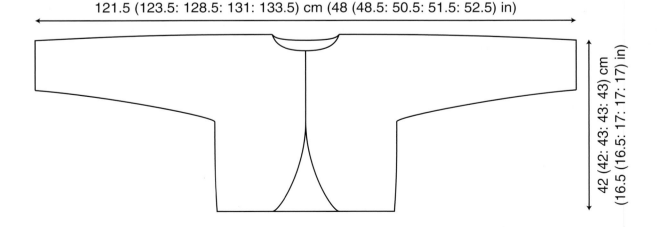

BRIDGET
MARTIN STOREY

This cardigan, knitted up here in black and white, takes us back to winter holidays in the 50's. The playful motifs and concertina-like geometrics are reminders of the paper cut-outs children make before Christmas to decorate the classroom windows. The black and white is tempered here by the pink blouse, which softens the look.

YARN

	XS	S	M	L	XL	
To fit bust	81	86	91	97	102	cm
	32	34	36	38	40	in

Rowan Yorkshire Tweed 4 ply

A Whiskers 283						
	9	10	10	11	12	x 25gm
B Desiccated 263						
	7	7	7	8	8	x 25gm

NEEDLES

1 pair 2³/₄ mm (no 12) (US 2) needles
1 pair 3¹/₄ mm (no 10) (US 3) needles

BUTTONS – 7 x 00315

TENSION

30 sts and 36 rows to 10 cm measured over patterned stocking stitch using 3¹/₄ mm (US 3) needles.

BACK

Cast on 121 (129: 137: 145: 153) sts using 2³/₄ mm (US 2) needles and yarn A.
Row 1 (RS): K1, *P1, K1, rep from * to end.
Row 2: As row 1.
These 2 rows form moss st.
Work in moss st for a further 11 rows, ending with a RS row.
Row 14 (WS): Moss st 6 (6: 5: 5: 4) sts, M1, *moss st 12 (13: 14: 15: 16) sts, M1, rep from * to last 7 (6: 6: 5: 5) sts, moss st to end.
131 (139: 147: 155: 163) sts.
Change to 3¹/₄ mm (US 3) needles.
Starting and ending rows as indicated, using the **fairisle** technique as described on the information page and **repeating chart rows 1 to 6 only,** cont in patt from chart, which is worked entirely in st st beg with a K row, as folls:
Dec 1 st at each end of 9th and every foll 6th row to 121 (129: 137: 145: 153) sts, then on every foll 4th row until 113 (121: 129: 137: 145) sts rem.
Work 9 rows, ending with a WS row.
Inc 1 st at each end of next and every foll 6th row until there are 131 (139: 147: 155: 163) sts, taking inc sts into patt.
Cont straight until back measures approx 35 (36: 36: 37: 37) cm, ending after chart row 6 and with a WS row.
Now working chart rows 7 to 12 **once only** and then repeating chart rows 13 to 52 **throughout,** cont as folls:
Work 4 rows, ending with a WS row.
Shape armholes
Keeping patt correct, cast off 6 (7: 7: 8: 8) sts at beg of next 2 rows. 119 (125: 133: 139: 147) sts.
Dec 1 st at each end of next 5 (5: 7: 7: 9) rows, then on foll 3 (4: 5: 6: 7) alt rows, then on every foll 4th row until 99 (103: 105: 109: 111) sts rem.
Cont straight until armhole measures 20 (20: 21: 21: 22) cm, ending with a WS row.
Shape shoulders and back neck
Cast off 9 (9: 9: 10: 10) sts at beg of next 2 rows.
81 (85: 87: 89: 91) sts.
Next row (RS): Cast off 9 (9: 9: 10: 10) sts, patt until there are 12 (13: 14: 13: 14) sts on right needle and turn, leaving rem sts on a holder.
Work each side of neck separately.
Cast off 4 sts at beg of next row.
Cast off rem 8 (9: 10: 9: 10) sts.
With RS facing, rejoin yarns to rem sts, cast off centre 39 (41: 41: 43: 43) sts, patt to end.
Complete to match first side, reversing shapings.

LEFT FRONT

Cast on 69 (73: 77: 81: 85) sts using 2³/₄ mm (US 2) needles and yarn A.
Work in moss st as given for back for 13 rows, ending with a RS row.
Row 14 (WS): Moss st 8 sts and slip these sts onto a holder, moss st 6 sts, M1, *moss st 12 (13: 14: 15: 16) sts, M1, rep from * to last 7 sts, moss st to end. 66 (70: 74: 78: 82) sts.
Change to 3¹/₄ mm (US 3) needles.
Starting and ending rows as indicated and **repeating chart rows 1 to 6 only,** cont in patt from chart as folls:
Dec 1 st at beg of 9th and every foll 6th row to 61 (65: 69: 73: 77) sts, then on every foll 4th row until 57 (61: 65: 69: 73) sts rem.
Work 9 rows, ending with a WS row.
Inc 1 st at beg of next and every foll 6th row until there are 66 (70: 74: 78: 82) sts, taking inc sts into patt.
Cont straight until left front measures approx 34 (35: 35: 36: 36) cm, ending after chart row 6 and with a WS row.
Now working chart rows 7 to 12 **once only** and then repeating chart rows 13 to 52 **throughout,** cont as folls:
Work 4 rows, ending with a WS row.
Shape armhole
Keeping patt correct, cast off 6 (7: 7: 8: 8) sts at beg of next row. 60 (63: 67: 70: 74) sts.
Work 1 row.
Dec 1 st at armhole edge of next 5 (5: 7: 7: 9) rows, then on foll 3 (4: 5: 6: 7) alt rows, then on every foll 4th row until 50 (52: 53: 55: 56) sts rem.
Cont straight until 21 (21: 21: 23: 23) rows less have been worked than on back to start of shoulder shaping, ending with a RS row.
Shape neck
Keeping patt correct, cast off 8 (9: 9: 9: 9) sts at beg of next row. 42 (43: 44: 46: 47) sts.
Dec 1 st at neck edge of next 12 rows, then on foll 4 (4: 4: 5: 5) alt rows, ending with a WS row. 26 (27: 28: 29: 30) sts.
Shape shoulder
Cast off 9 (9: 9: 10: 10) sts at beg of next and foll alt row.
Work 1 row.
Cast off rem 8 (9: 10: 9: 10) sts.

RIGHT FRONT

Cast on 69 (73: 77: 81: 85) sts using 2³/₄ mm (US 2) needles and yarn A.
Work in moss st as given for back for 4 rows,

ending with a WS row.

Row 5 (RS): Moss st 2 sts, K2tog, yfwd (to
make a buttonhole), moss st to end.

Work in moss st for a further 8 rows, ending
with a RS row.

Row 14 (WS): Moss st 6 sts, M1, *moss st
12 (13: 14: 15: 16) sts, M1, rep from * to last
15 sts, moss st to last 8 sts and turn, leaving
rem 8 sts on a holder. 66 (70: 74: 78: 82) sts.
Change to 3¹/₄ mm (US 3) needles.
Starting and ending rows as indicated and
repeating chart rows 1 to 6 only, cont in patt
from chart as folls:
Dec 1 st at end of 9th and every foll 6th row to
61 (65: 69: 73: 77) sts, then on every foll 4th
row until 57 (61: 65: 69: 73) sts rem.
Complete to match left front, reversing shapings.

SLEEVES (both alike)

Cast on 63 (63: 65: 67: 67) sts using 2³/₄ mm
(US 2) needles and yarn A.
Work in moss st as given for back for 13 rows,
ending with a RS row.

Row 14 (WS): Moss st 7 (7: 8: 9: 9) sts, M1,
*moss st 16 sts, M1, rep from * to last 8 (8: 9:
10: 10) sts, moss st to end.
67 (67: 69: 71: 71) sts.
Change to 3¹/₄ mm (US 3) needles.
Starting and ending rows as indicated and
repeating chart rows 1 to 6 only, cont in patt
from chart as folls:
Inc 1 st at each end of 7th (7th: 5th: 5th: 5th)
and every foll 8th (8th: 8th: 8th: 6th) row to
87 (97: 103: 105: 89) sts, then on every foll
10th (10th: -: -: 8th) row until there are 97 (99:
-: -: 109) sts, taking inc sts into patt.
Cont straight until sleeve measures approx
43 (43: 44: 44: 44) cm, ending after chart row 6
and with a WS row.
Now working chart rows 7 to 12 **once only** and
then repeating chart rows 13 to 52 **throughout,**
cont as folls:
Work 4 rows, ending with a WS row.

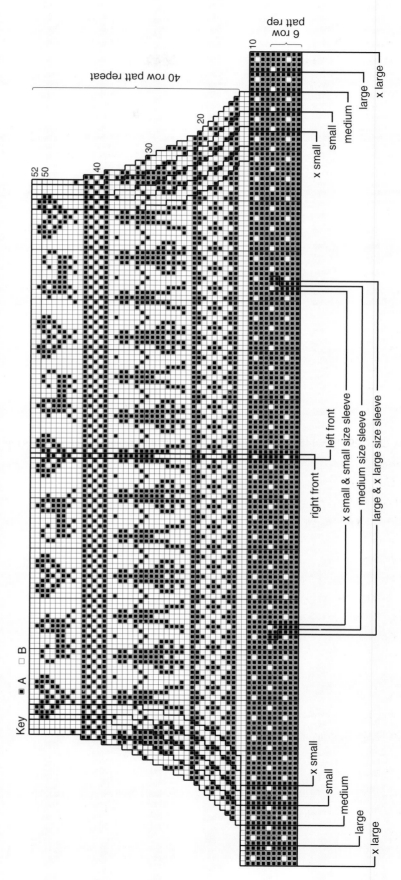

33

Shape top

Keeping patt correct, cast off 6 (7: 7: 8: 8) sts at beg of next 2 rows. 85 (85: 89: 89: 93) sts.

Dec 1 st at each end of next 5 rows, then on foll 4 alt rows, then on every foll 4th row until 57 (57: 61: 61: 65) sts rem.

Work 1 row, ending with a WS row.

Dec 1 st at each end of next and every foll alt row to 45 sts, then on foll 7 rows, ending with a WS row.

Cast off rem 31 sts.

MAKING UP

PRESS as described on the information page.

Join both shoulder seams using back stitch, or mattress stitch if preferred.

Button band

Slip 8 sts left on left front holder onto 2³/₄ mm (US 2) needles and rejoin yarn A with RS facing.

Cont in moss st as set until button band, when slightly stretched, fits up left front opening edge to neck shaping, ending with a WS row. Break yarn and leave sts on a holder.

Mark positions for 7 buttons on this band – first to come level with buttonhole already worked in right front, last to come just above neck shaping and rem 5 buttons evenly spaced between.

Buttonhole band

Slip 8 sts left on right front holder onto 2³/₄ mm (US 2) needles and rejoin yarn A with WS facing.

Cont in moss st as set until buttonhole band, when slightly stretched, fits up right front opening edge to neck shaping, ending with a WS row and with the addition of a further 5 buttonholes worked to correspond with positions marked for buttons on left front as folls:

Buttonhole row (RS): K1, P1, K2tog, yfwd, (K1, P1) twice.

When band is complete, do NOT break yarn.

Slip st bands in place.

Neckband

With RS facing, using 2³/₄ mm (US 2) needles and yarn A, moss st 8 sts of buttonhole band, pick up and knit 30 (31: 31: 33: 33) sts up right side of neck, 47 (49: 49: 51: 51) sts from back, and 30 (31: 31: 33: 33) sts down left side of neck, then moss st 8 sts of button band. 123 (127: 127: 133: 133) sts.

Work in moss st as set by bands for 1 row, ending with a WS row.

Row 2 (RS): K1, P1, K2tog, yfwd, moss st to end.

Work in moss st for a further 2 rows, ending with a RS row.

Cast off in moss st (on WS).

See information page for finishing instructions, setting in sleeves using the set-in method.

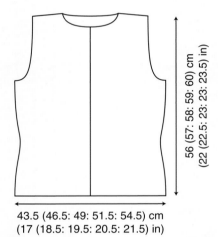

43.5 (46.5: 49: 51.5: 54.5) cm
(17 (18.5: 19.5: 20.5: 21.5) in)

56 (57: 58: 59: 60) cm
(22 (22.5: 22.5: 23: 23.5) in)

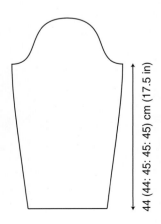

44 (44: 45: 45: 45) cm (17.5 in)

CLARK

KIM HARGREAVES

The big roll neck and enveloping look of this jumper has a true 50's and 60's feel with the smouldering mood of French film stars. It's a look encapsulated by the singer Jean Paul Belmondo. The seamed effect, marking the transition between the body and the rib, is a clever finishing touch.

YARN

	S	M	L	XL	XXL	
To fit chest	97	102	107	112	117	cm
	38	40	42	44	46	in

Rowan Yorkshire Tweed DK

| | 13 | 13 | 14 | 14 | 15 | x 50gm |

(photographed in Goose 352)

NEEDLES

1 pair 3³/₄ mm (no 9) (US 5) needles
1 pair 4mm (no 8) (US 6) needles
3³/₄ mm (no 9) (US 5) circular needle
4mm (no 8) (US 6) circular needle

TENSION

20 sts and 28 rows to 10 cm measured over
stocking stitch using 4mm (US 6) needles.

BACK

Lower section

Cast on 113 (117: 123: 127: 133) sts using
3³/₄ mm (US 5) needles.

Row 1 (RS): P0 (2: 0: 2: 0), *K3, P2, rep from
* to last 3 (0: 3: 0: 3) sts, K3 (0: 3: 0: 3).

Row 2: K0 (2: 0: 2: 0), *P3, K2, rep from * to
last 3 (0: 3: 0: 3) sts, P3 (0: 3: 0: 3).

These 2 rows form rib.

Cont in rib for a further 22 rows, ending with a
WS row.

Cast off in rib.

Main section

With WS facing (so that ridge is formed on RS
of work) and using 4mm (US 6) needles, pick
up and knit 113 (117: 123: 127: 133) sts across
cast-off edge of lower section.

Beg with a K row, cont in st st until back
measures 40 (40: 41: 41: 42) cm from cast-on
edge of lower section, ending with a WS row.

Shape armholes

Cast off 4 sts at beg of next 2 rows.

105 (109: 115: 119: 125) sts.

Next row (RS): K2, K3tog, K to last 5 sts,
K3tog tbl, K2.

Next row: Purl.

Rep last 2 rows twice more.

93 (97: 103: 107: 113) sts.

Cont straight until armhole measures 20 (21: 21: 22: 22) cm, ending with a WS row.**

Cont in ridge patt as folls:

Row 1 (RS): Purl.

Rows 2 and 3: Knit.

Row 4: Purl.

These 4 rows form ridge patt.

Work in ridge patt for a further 6 rows, ending with a WS row.

Shape back neck

Next row (RS): Patt 29 (30: 33: 34: 36) sts and turn, leaving rem sts on a holder.

Work each side of neck separately.

Cast off 4 sts at beg of next row.

Shape shoulder

Leave rem 25 (26: 29: 30: 32) sts on a holder.

With RS facing, rejoin yarn to rem sts, cast off centre 35 (37: 37: 39: 41) sts, patt to end.

Complete to match first side, reversing shapings.

FRONT

Work as given for back to **, ending with a WS row.

Beg with row 1, now work in ridge patt as given for back and cont as folls:

Shape neck

Next row (RS): Patt 30 (31: 34: 35: 37) sts and turn, leaving rem sts on a holder.

Work each side of neck separately.

Dec 1 st at neck edge on next 4 rows, then on foll alt row.

25 (26: 29: 30: 32) sts.

Work 5 rows, ending with a WS row.

Shape shoulder

Leave rem 25 (26: 29: 30: 32) sts on a holder.

With RS facing, rejoin yarn to rem sts, cast off centre 33 (35: 35: 37: 39) sts, patt to end.

Complete to match first side, reversing shapings.

SLEEVES (both alike)

Lower section

Cast on 63 (63: 65: 67: 67) sts using 3³/₄ mm (US 5) needles.

Row 1 (RS): P0 (0: 1: 2: 2), *K3, P2, rep from * to last 3 (3: 4: 5: 5) sts, K3, P0 (0: 1: 2: 2).

Row 2: K0 (0: 1: 2: 2), *P3, K2, rep from * to last 3 (3: 4: 5: 5) sts, P3, K0 (0: 1: 2: 2).

These 2 rows form rib.

Cont in rib for a further 30 rows, ending with a WS row.

Cast off in rib.

Main section

With WS facing (so that ridge is formed on RS of work) and using 4mm (US 6) needles, pick up and knit 63 (63: 65: 67: 67) sts across cast-off edge of lower section.

Beg with a K row, cont in st st as folls:

Work 2 rows, ending with a WS row.

Next row (RS): K2, M1, K to last 2 sts, M1, K2.

Working all increases as set by last row, inc 1 st at each end of every foll 6th row to 91 (85: 91: 93: 93) sts, then on every foll 4th row until there are 101 (105: 105: 109: 109) sts.

Cont straight until sleeve measures 52 (53: 53: 54: 54) cm from cast-on edge of lower section, ending with a WS row.

Shape top

Cast off 4 sts at beg of next 2 rows.

93 (97: 97: 101: 101) sts.

Next row (RS): K2, K3tog, K to last 5 sts, K3tog tbl, K2.

Work 3 rows.

Rep last 4 rows twice more.

Cast off rem 81 (85: 85: 89: 89) sts.

MAKING UP

PRESS as described on the information page.

Join shoulder seams as folls: holding back and front WS together and working with front towards you, cast off sts of each shoulder edge together, taking one st from front together with one st from back.

Collar

With RS facing and using 3³/₄ mm (US 5) circular needle, starting and ending at left shoulder seam, pick up and knit 13 sts down left side of neck, 32 (35: 35: 37: 39) sts from front, 13 sts up right side of neck, then 42 (44: 44: 47: 50) sts from back.

100 (105: 105: 110: 115) sts.

Round 1 (RS): *K2, P3, rep from * to end.

This round forms rib.

Cont in rib until collar measures 8 cm.

Change to 4mm (US 6) circular needle.

Cont in rib until collar measures 20 cm.

Cast off in rib.

See information page for finishing instructions, setting in sleeves using the shallow set-in method.

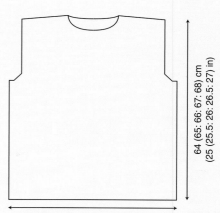

56.5 (58.5: 61.5: 63.5: 66.5) cm
(22 (23: 24: 25: 26) in)

64 (65: 66: 67: 68) cm
(25 (25.5: 26: 26.5: 27) in)

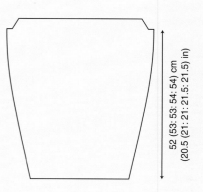

52 (53: 53: 54: 54) cm
(20.5 (21: 21: 21.5: 21.5) in)

AIMEE
KIM HARGREAVES

This fine, airy jumper creates a sense of light and space.
It's knitted loose enough to show glimpses of the fabric
underneath, creating a layered effect that's enhanced by
the bands. The smooth cotton of the Liberty-style floral
perfectly sets off the hazy surface of the knitwear, echoing
the autumn light filtering through the ancient trees.

AIMEE
KIM HARGREAVES

YARN

	XS	S	M	L	XL	
To fit bust	81	86	91	97	102	cm
	32	34	36	38	40	in

Rowan Kid Silk Haze

| | 4 | 4 | 4 | 5 | 5 | x 25gm |

(photographed in Blushes 583)

NEEDLES

1 pair 3mm (no 11) (US 2/3) needles
1 pair 3$^{1}/_{4}$ mm (no 10) (US 3) needles
1 pair 3$^{3}/_{4}$ mm (no 9) (US 5) needles
1 pair 4$^{1}/_{2}$ mm (no 7) (US 7) needles

RIBBON – 2.30 m of 3.5 cm wide ribbon

TENSION

20 sts and 20 rows to 10 cm measured over pattern using a combination of 3$^{3}/_{4}$ mm (US 5) and yarn DOUBLE and 4$^{1}/_{2}$ mm (US 7) needles and yarn SINGLE.

BACK

Cast on 82 (86: 92: 96: 102) sts using 3$^{1}/_{4}$ mm (US 3) needles and yarn DOUBLE.
Beg with a K row, work in st st for 10 rows, ending with a WS row.
Change to 3$^{3}/_{4}$ mm (US 5) needles.
Row 11 (fold line row) (RS): K1, *sl 1, K1, psso, yfwd, rep from * to last st, K1.**
Beg with a P row, work in st st for 11 rows **and at same time** dec 1 st at each end of 6th and foll 4th row, ending with a WS row.
78 (82: 88: 92: 98) sts.
***Cont in patt as folls:
Change to 4$^{1}/_{2}$ mm (US 7) needles and yarn SINGLE.
Row 1 (RS): Knit.
Row 2: K1, *yfwd, sl 1, K1, psso, rep from * to last st, K1,
Row 3: K2tog, K1, *yfwd, sl 1, K1, psso, rep from * to last 3 sts, K1, K2tog.
76 (80: 86: 90: 96) sts.

Rows 4 and 5: K2, *yfwd, sl 1, K1, psso, rep from * to last 2 sts, K2.
Row 6: Purl.
Change to 3$^{3}/_{4}$ mm (US 5) needles and yarn DOUBLE.
Beg with a K row, work in st st for 6 rows **and at same time** dec 1 st at each end of next and foll 4th row, ending with a WS row.
72 (76: 82: 86: 92) sts.
Last 12 rows form lace stripe and st st patt and start side seam shaping.
Cont in patt, dec 1 st at each end of 3rd row.
70 (74: 80: 84: 90) sts.
Work 9 rows, ending with a WS row.
Inc 1 st at each end of next and every foll 4th row until there are 82 (86: 92: 96: 102) sts, taking inc sts into patt.
Work 7 (9: 9: 11: 11) rows, ending with a WS row. (Back should measure 32 (33: 33: 34: 34) cm **from fold line row**.)
Shape armholes
Keeping patt correct, cast off 3 (4: 4: 5: 5) sts at beg of next 2 rows.
76 (78: 84: 86: 92) sts.
Dec 1 st at each end of next 5 (5: 7: 7: 9) rows, then on foll 3 alt rows.
60 (62: 64: 66: 68) sts.
Work a further 9 (7: 5: 3: 1) rows, ending after patt row 2 and with a WS row.
Now repeating last row **only** (to complete work in lace patt), cont straight until armhole measures 20 (20: 21: 21: 22) cm, ending with a WS row.
Shape shoulders and back neck
Cast off 4 (4: 4: 4: 5) sts at beg of next 2 rows.
52 (54: 56: 58: 58) sts.
Next row (RS): Cast off 4 (4: 4: 4: 5) sts, patt until there are 8 (8: 9: 9: 8) sts on right needle and turn, leaving rem sts on a holder.
Work each side of neck separately.
Cast off 4 sts at beg of next row.
Cast off rem 4 (4: 5: 5: 4) sts.
With RS facing, rejoin yarn to rem sts, cast off

centre 28 (30: 30: 32: 32) sts, patt to end.
Complete to match first side, reversing shapings.

FRONT

Work as given for Back to **.
Beg with a P row, work in st st for 1 row, ending with a WS row.
Divide for ribbon opening
Next row (RS): K40 (42: 45: 47: 50) and slip these sts onto a holder, cast off 2 sts, K to end.
Work 7 rows on this last set of 40 (42: 45: 47: 50) sts, dec 1 st at end of 4th of these rows and ending with a WS row.
39 (41: 44: 46: 49) sts.
Break yarn and leave sts on another holder.
With **WS** facing, rejoin yarn to 40 (42: 45: 47: 50) sts left on first holder, P to end.
Work 6 rows on these sts, dec 1 st at beg of 3rd of these rows and ending with a WS row.
39 (41: 44: 46: 49) sts.
Join sections
Next row (RS): K2tog, K rem 37 (39: 42: 44: 47) sts, turn and cast on 2 sts, turn and K across first 37 (39: 42: 44: 47) sts left on holder, K2tog.
78 (82: 88: 92: 98) sts.
Work 1 row, ending with a WS row.
Work as given for back from *** until 6 (6: 6: 8: 8) rows less have been worked than on back to start of shoulder shaping, ending with a WS row.
Shape front neck
Next row (RS): Patt 17 (17: 18: 19: 20) sts and turn, leaving rem sts on a holder.
Work each side of neck separately.
Dec 1 st at neck edge of next 4 rows, then on foll 0 (0: 0: 1: 1) alt row.
13 (13: 14: 14: 15) sts.
Work 1 row, ending with a WS row.
Shape shoulder
Cast off 4 (4: 4: 4: 5) sts at beg of next and foll alt row **and at same time** dec 1 st at neck edge

of next row.

Work 1 row.

Cast off rem 4 (4: 5: 5: 4) sts.

With RS facing, rejoin yarn to rem sts, cast off centre 26 (28: 28: 28: 28) sts, patt to end.

Complete to match first side, reversing shapings.

SLEEVES (both alike)

Cast on 46 (46: 48: 50: 50) sts using 3¼ mm (US 3) needles and yarn DOUBLE.

Work in garter st for 4 rows, ending with a WS row.

Change to 3¾ mm mm (US 5) needles.

Beg with a K row, work in st st for 4 rows, ending with a WS row.

Cont in patt as folls:

Change to 4½ mm (US 7) needles and yarn SINGLE.

Row 1 (RS): Knit.

Rows 2 to 5: K1, *yfwd, sl 1, K1, psso, rep from * to last st, K1,

Row 6: Purl.

Change to 3¾ mm (US 5) needles and yarn DOUBLE.

Beg with a K row, work in st st for 6 rows, inc 1 st at each end of first of these rows and ending with a WS row. 48 (48: 50: 52: 52) sts.

Last 12 rows form lace stripe and st st patt and start sleeve shaping.

Cont in patt, shaping sides by inc 1 st at each end of 7th (5th: 5th: 5th: 3rd) and every foll 12th (10th: 10th: 10th: 8th) row to 54 (56: 56: 58: 56) sts, then on every foll 14th (12th: 12th: 12th: 10th) row until there are 58 (60: 62: 64: 66) sts, taking inc sts into patt.

Cont straight until sleeve measures 43 (43: 44: 44: 44) cm, ending with a WS row.

Shape top

Keeping patt correct, cast off 3 (4: 4: 5: 5) sts at beg of next 2 rows. 52 (52: 54: 54: 56) sts.

Dec 1 st at each end of next 3 rows, then on foll 2 alt rows, then on every foll 4th row until 36 (36: 38: 38: 40) sts rem.

Work 1 row, ending with a WS row.

Dec 1 st at each end of next and every foll alt row to 32 sts, then on foll row, ending with a WS row.

30 sts.

Cast off 4 sts at beg of next 2 rows.

Cast off rem 22 sts.

MAKING UP

PRESS as described on the information page.

Join right shoulder seam using back stitch, or mattress stitch if preferred.

Neckband

With RS facing, using 3mm (US 2/3) needles and yarn SINGLE, pick up and knit 10 (10: 10: 12: 12) sts down left side of neck, 26 (28: 28: 28: 28) sts from front, 10 (10: 10: 12: 12) sts up right side of neck, then 36 (38: 38: 40: 40) sts from back.

82 (86: 86: 92: 92) sts.

Beg with a K row, work in rev st st for 4 rows, ending with a RS row.

Cast off **very loosely** knitwise (on WS).

See information page for finishing instructions, setting in sleeves using the set-in method. Fold first 10 rows to inside around lower edge of back and front and slip stitch in place. Thread ribbon through this casing.

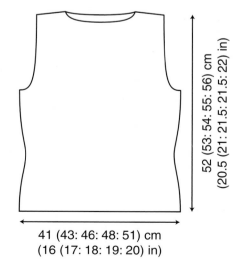

41 (43: 46: 48: 51) cm
(16 (17: 18: 19: 20) in)

52 (53: 54: 55: 56) cm
(20.5 (21: 21.5: 21.5: 22) in)

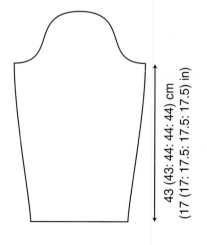

43 (43: 44: 44: 44) cm
(17 (17: 17.5: 17.5: 17.5) in)

ELISE

KIM HARGREAVES

This design, with its low neckline, has a glamorous, even risque look. The diagonal line is given softness by the crinkled edge. The textured handle of the tweed is complemented here by the smooth fabric of the skirt, which continues the figure-hugging line. The side fastening gives a chance to use an eye-catching item of your own choice.

YARN

	XS	S	M	L	XL	
To fit bust	81	86	91	97	102	cm
	32	34	36	38	40	in

Rowan Felted Tweed

	6	7	7	8	8	x 50gm

(photographed in Sigh 148)

NEEDLES

1 pair 3¼ mm (no 10) (US 3) needles
1 pair 3¾ mm (no 9) (US 5) needles

EXTRAS – 1m of narrow ribbon and decorative pin fastener

TENSION

23 sts and 32 rows to 10 cm measured over stocking stitch using 3¾ mm (US 5) needles.

BACK

Cast on 91 (97: 103: 109: 115) sts using 3¼ mm (US 3) needles.
Work in garter st for 4 rows, ending with a WS row.
Change to 3¾ mm (US 5) needles.
Beg with a K row, work in st st for 8 rows, ending with a WS row.
Next row (RS): K2, K2tog, K to last 4 sts, K2tog tbl, K2.
Working all sides seam decreases as set by last row, cont in st st, dec 1 st at each end of every foll 12th row until 85 (91: 97: 103: 109) sts rem.
Cont straight until back measures 16 (17: 17: 18: 18) cm, ending with a WS row.
Next row (RS): K2, M1, K to last 2 sts, M1, K2.
Working all side seam increases as set by last row, inc 1 st at each end of every foll 10th row until there are 97 (103: 109: 115: 121) sts.
Work 17 rows, ending with a WS row. (Back should measure 37 (38: 38: 39: 39) cm.)

Shape armholes

Cast off 4 (5: 5: 6: 6) sts at beg of next 2 rows.
89 (93: 99: 103: 109) sts.

Dec 1 st at each end of next 3 (3: 5: 5: 7) rows,
then on foll 3 (4: 4: 5: 5) alt rows.
77 (79: 81: 83: 85) sts.

Cont straight until armhole measures 21 (21: 22: 22: 23) cm, ending with a WS row.

Shape shoulders and back neck

Next row (RS): Cast off 6 sts, K until there are 14 (14: 15: 15: 16) sts on right needle and turn, leaving rem sts on a holder.

Work each side of neck separately.

Dec 1 st at beg of next row.

Cast off 6 sts at beg and dec 1 st at end of next row.

Dec 1 st at beg of next row.

Cast off rem 5 (5: 6: 6: 7) sts.

With RS facing, rejoin yarn to rem sts, cast off centre 37 (39: 39: 41: 41) sts, K to end.

Complete to match first side, reversing shapings.

LEFT FRONT

Cast on 79 (82: 85: 88: 91) sts using 3¼ mm (US 3) needles.

Work in garter st for 4 rows, ending with a WS row.

Change to 3¾ mm (US 5) needles.

Row 5 (RS): Knit.

Row 6: K15, P to end.

Last 2 rows set the sts – front opening edge 15 sts in garter st and rem sts in st st.

Keeping sts correct as set, work 6 rows, ending with a WS row.

Working all sides seam decreases as given for back, dec 1 st at beg of next and every foll 12th row until 76 (79: 82: 85: 88) sts rem.

Cont straight until 6 rows less have been worked than on back to first side seam inc, ending with a WS row.

Next row (RS): Knit.

Next row: K1, (take yarn round needle and draw loop through st on right needle as though to K a st) 4 times (to create short chain), K14, P to end.

Rep last 2 rows once more.

Next row: Knit.

Next row: K1, (take yarn round needle and draw loop through st on right needle as though to K a st) 4 times (to create short chain), K14, wrap next st (by slipping next st to right needle, taking yarn to opposite side of work between needles and then slipping same st back onto left needle – when working back across sts work the wrapped loop tog with the wrapped st), turn, K15, turn, K1, (take yarn round needle and draw loop through st on right needle as though to K a st) 4 times (to create short chain), K14, P to end.

Last 4 rows set the sts – front opening edge 15 sts as frill edging and rem sts in st st.

Shape front slope

Next row (RS): K2, M1, K to last 19 sts, K2tog tbl, K17.
76 (79: 82: 85: 88) sts.

This row sets side seam increases and front slope decreases.

Working all increases and decreases as set by last row, dec 1 st at front slope edge of 2nd and foll 12 (14: 13: 15: 13) alt rows, then on 6 (5: 5: 4: 5) foll 4th rows and at same time inc 1 st at side seam edge on 10th and every foll 10th row.
62 (64: 68: 70: 74) sts.

Dec 1 st at front slope edge only on 4th (4th: 2nd: 2nd: 2nd) and every foll 4th row until 58 (60: 64: 66: 70) sts rem.

Work 1 (1: 3: 3: 3) rows, ending with a WS row. (Left front now matches back to beg of armhole shaping.)

Shape armhole

Keeping sts correct, cast off 4 (5: 5: 6: 6) sts at beg and dec 0 (0: 1: 1: 1) st at front slope edge of next row.
54 (55: 58: 59: 63) sts.

Work 1 row.

Dec 1 st at armhole edge of next 3 (3: 5: 5: 7) rows, then on foll 3 (4: 4: 5: 5) alt rows and at same time dec 1 st at front slope edge of next (next: 3rd: 3rd: 3rd) and every foll 4th row.
45 (45: 46: 45: 47) sts.

Dec 1 st at front slope edge only on 4th (2nd: 2nd: 4th: 2nd) and every foll 4th row until 33 (33: 34: 34: 35) sts rem.

Cont straight until left front matches back to start of shoulder shaping, ending with a WS row.

Shape shoulder

Cast off 6 sts at beg of next and foll alt row, then 5 (5: 6: 6: 7) sts at beg of foll alt row.
16 sts.

Cont as set on these 16 sts until shorter edge measures 9 (9.5: 9.5: 10: 10) cm.

Cast off.

RIGHT FRONT

Cast on 79 (82: 85: 88: 91) sts using 3¼ mm (US 3) needles.

Rows 1 and 2: Knit.

Row 3 (RS): K1, (take yarn round needle and draw loop through st on right needle as though to K a st) 4 times (to create short chain), K14, wrap next st, turn, K15, turn, K1, (take yarn round needle and draw loop through st on right needle as though to K a st) 4 times (to create short chain), K to end.

Row 4: Knit.

Change to 3¾ mm (US 5) needles.

Row 5 (RS): K1, (take yarn round needle and draw loop through st on right needle as though to K a st) 4 times (to create short chain), K to end.

Row 6: P to last 15 sts, K15.

Row 7: K1, (take yarn round needle and draw loop through st on right needle as though to K a st) 4 times (to create short chain), K14, wrap next st, turn, K15, turn, K1, (take yarn round needle and draw loop through st on right needle as though to K a st) 4 times (to create short chain), K to end.

Row 8: As row 6.

Last 4 rows set the sts – front opening edge 15 sts as frill edging and rem sts in st st.

Keeping sts correct as set, work 4 rows, ending with a WS row.

Working all sides seam decreases as given for back, dec 1 st at end of next and every foll 12th row until 76 (79: 82: 85: 88) sts rem.

Cont straight until right front measures 16 (17: 17: 18: 18) cm, ending with a WS row.

Shape front slope

Next row (RS): Patt 15 sts, K2, K2tog, K to last 2 sts, M1, K2.

76 (79: 82: 85: 88) sts.

This row sets front slope decreases.

Complete to match left front, reversing shapings.

SLEEVES (both alike)

Cast on 51 (51: 53: 55: 55) sts using 3¼ mm (US 3) needles.

Work in garter st for 4 rows, ending with a WS row.

Change to 3¾ mm (US 5) needles.

Beg with a K row, work in st st for 6 rows, ending with a WS row.

Next row (RS): K2, M1, K to last 2 sts, M1, K2.

Working all increases as set by last row, inc 1 st at each end of every foll 8th (8th: 8th: 8th: 6th) row to 67 (77: 77: 79: 63) sts, then on every foll 10th (-: 10th: 10th: 8th) row until there are 75 (-: 79: 81: 83) sts.

Cont straight until sleeve measures 38 (38: 39: 39: 39) cm, ending with a WS row.

Shape top

Cast off 4 (5: 5: 6: 6) sts at beg of next 2 rows.

67 (67: 69: 69: 71) sts.

Dec 1 st at each end of next 5 rows, then on foll 2 alt rows, then on every foll 4th row until 39 (39: 41: 41: 43) sts rem.

Work 1 row, ending with a WS row.

Dec 1 st at each end of next and every foll alt row to 35 sts, then on foll 7 rows, ending with a WS row.

Cast off rem 21 sts.

MAKING UP

PRESS as described on the information page.

Join both shoulder seams using back stitch, or mattress stitch if preferred. Join cast-off ends of frill strips, then sew shorter edge to back neck, easing in fullness.

Cuffs (both alike)

Cast on 16 sts using 3¾ mm (US 5) needles.

Rows 1 and 2: Knit.

Row 3 (RS): K1, (take yarn round needle and draw loop through st on right needle as though to K a st) 4 times (to create short chain), K14, wrap next st, turn, K15, turn, K1, (take yarn round needle and draw loop through st on right needle as though to K a st) 4 times (to create short chain), K to end.

Row 4: Knit.

Row 5: K1, (take yarn round needle and draw loop through st on right needle as though to K a st) 4 times (to create short chain), K to end.

Row 6: Knit.

Last 4 rows form patt.

Cont in patt until shorter edge of cuff fits along cast-on edge of sleeve, ending with a WS row. Cast off.

Sew cuffs to lower edges of sleeves.

See information page for finishing instructions, setting in sleeves using the set-in method.

Cut ribbon into 2 equal lengths and attach one length to inside of left front opening edge, 16 sts on from actual edge and level with start of front slope shaping. Attach other length to inside of right side seam, level with first length. Tie ribbons together to hold left front in place, and fasten right front with a decorative pin.

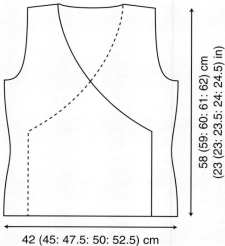
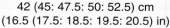
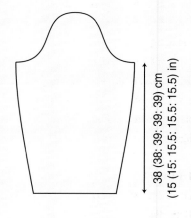

58 (59: 60: 61: 62) cm
(23 (23: 23.5: 24: 24.5) in)

42 (45: 47.5: 50: 52.5) cm
(16.5 (17.5: 18.5: 19.5: 20.5) in)

38 (38: 39: 39: 39) cm
(15 (15: 15.5: 15.5: 15.5) in)

TYROLEAN
SARAH DALLAS

Waist-length, figure-hugging cardigans were hugely
popular in the 1940's, often knitted in sugar sweet
colours and complex patterns. This version, knitted in
rich dark colours and brightened by rows of
embroidered flowers, is the epitome of sophisticated
chic, when teamed with a classic pencil skirt. The hat
and small Gladstone bag complete the look.

YARN

	XS	S	M	L	XL	
To fit bust	81	86	91	97	102	cm
	32	34	36	38	40	in

Rowan Yorkshire Tweed DK

A Rowdy	355					
	9	10	10	11	11	x 50gm
B Frolic 350						
	1	1	1	1	1	x 50gm
C Frog 349						
	1	1	1	1	1	x 50gm
D Lime Leaf 348						
	1	1	1	1	1	x 50gm

NEEDLES

1 pair 3¼ mm (no 10) (US 3) needles
1 pair 4mm (no 8) (US 6) needles

BUTTONS – 7 x 00320

TENSION

20 sts and 28 rows to 10 cm measured over stocking stitch using 4mm (US 6) needles.

SPECIAL ABBREVIATIONS

MB = K into front, back, front, back and front again of next st, turn, P5, turn, sl 2, K3tog, pass 2 slipped sts over.

BACK

Cast on 82 (86: 90: 94: 102) sts using 3¼ mm (US 3) needles and yarn B.
Break off yarn B and join in yarn A.
Row 1 (RS): K2, *P2, K2, rep from * to end.
Row 2: P2, *K2, P2, rep from * to end.
These 2 rows form rib.
Work in rib for 5 cm, dec (dec: inc: inc: dec) 1 st at end of last row and ending with a WS row.
81 (85: 91: 95: 101) sts.
Change to 4mm (US 6) needles.
Beg with a K row, cont in st st, shaping side seams by inc 1 st at each end of 3rd and every foll 12th row until there are 91 (95: 101: 105: 111) sts.

Cont straight until back measures 30 (31: 31: 32: 32) cm, ending with a WS row.

Shape armholes

Cast off 5 (6: 6: 7: 7) sts at beg of next 2 rows.
81 (83: 89: 91: 97) sts.
Dec 1 st at each end of next 5 (5: 7: 7: 9) rows, then on foll 2 alt rows, then on foll 4th row.
65 (67: 69: 71: 73) sts.
Cont straight until armhole measures 19 (19: 20: 20: 21) cm, ending with a WS row.

Shape shoulders and back neck

Cast off 6 sts at beg of next 2 rows.
53 (55: 57: 59: 61) sts.
Next row (RS): Cast off 6 sts, K until there are 9 (9: 10: 10: 11) sts on right needle and turn, leaving rem sts on a holder.
Work each side of neck separately.
Cast off 4 sts at beg of next row.
Cast off rem 5 (5: 6: 6: 7) sts.
With RS facing, rejoin yarn to rem sts, cast off centre 23 (25: 25: 27: 27) sts, K to end.
Complete to match first side, reversing shapings.

LEFT FRONT

Cast on 43 (43: 47: 47: 51) sts using 3¼ mm (US 3) needles and yarn B.
Break off yarn B and join in yarn A.
Row 1 (RS): *K2, P2, rep from * to last 3 sts, K3.
Row 2: K1, P2, *K2, P2, rep from * to end.
These 2 rows form rib.
Work in rib for 5 cm, dec (-: dec: inc: -) 2 (-: 1: 1: -) sts across last row and ending with a WS row. 41 (43: 46: 48: 51) sts.
Change to 4mm (US 6) needles.
Row 1 (RS): K to last 29 sts, MB, K5, MB, K9, MB, K5, MB, K6.
Row 2: Purl.
Row 3: Inc in first st, K to last 26 sts, MB, K15, MB, K9. 42 (44: 47: 49: 52) sts.
Row 4: Purl.
These 4 rows form patt and start side seam shaping.

Cont in patt, shaping side seam by inc 1 st at beg of 11th and every foll 12th row until there are 46 (48: 51: 53: 56) sts.
Cont straight until left front matches back to beg of armhole shaping, ending with a WS row.

Shape armhole

Keeping patt correct, cast off 5 (6: 6: 7: 7) sts at beg of next row.
41 (42: 45: 46: 49) sts.
Work 1 row.
Dec 1 st at armhole edge of next 5 (5: 7: 7: 9) rows, then on foll 2 alt rows, then on foll 4th row.
33 (34: 35: 36: 37) sts.
Cont straight until 17 (17: 17: 19: 19) rows less have been worked than on back to start of shoulder shaping, ending with a RS row.

Shape neck

Keeping patt correct, cast off 8 (9: 9: 9: 9) sts at beg of next row.
25 (25: 26: 27: 28) sts.
Dec 1 st at neck edge on next 5 rows, then on foll 2 (2: 2: 3: 3) alt rows, then on foll 4th row.
17 (17: 18: 18: 19) sts.
Work 3 rows, ending with a WS row.

Shape shoulder

Cast off 6 sts at beg of next and foll alt row.
Work 1 row.
Cast off rem 5 (5: 6: 6: 7) sts.

RIGHT FRONT

Cast on 43 (43: 47: 47: 51) sts using 3¼ mm (US 3) needles and yarn B.
Break off yarn B and join in yarn A.
Row 1 (RS): K3, *P2, K2, rep from * to end.
Row 2: P2, *K2, P2, rep from * to last st, K1.
These 2 rows form rib.
Work in rib for 5 cm, dec (-: dec: inc: -) 2 (-: 1: 1: -) sts across last row and ending with a WS row. 41 (43: 46: 48: 51) sts.
Change to 4mm (US 6) needles.
Row 1 (RS): K6, MB, K5, MB, K9, MB, K5, MB, K to end.
Row 2: Purl.

Row 3: K9, MB, K15, MB, K to last st, inc in last st. 42 (44: 47: 49: 52) sts.

Row 4: Purl.

These 4 rows form patt and start side seam shaping.

Cont in patt, shaping side seam by inc 1 st at end of 11th and every foll 12th row until there are 46 (48: 51: 53: 56) sts.

Complete to match left front, reversing shapings.

SLEEVES (both alike)

Cast on 46 (46: 50: 50: 50) sts using 3¼ mm (US 3) needles and yarn B.

Break off yarn B and join in yarn A.

Work in rib as given for back for 5 cm, inc (inc: dec: inc: inc) 1 st at end of last row and ending with a WS row. 47 (47: 49: 51: 51) sts.

Change to 4mm (US 6) needles.

Row 1 (RS): K15 (15: 16: 17: 17), MB, K15, MB, K to end.

Row 2: Purl.

Row 3: Inc in first st, K11 (11: 12: 13: 13), MB, K5, MB, K9, MB, K5, MB, K to last st, inc in last st. 49 (49: 51: 53: 53) sts.

Row 4: Purl.

These 4 rows form patt and start sleeve shaping.

Cont in patt, inc 1 st at each end of 9th (9th: 9th: 9th: 7th) and every foll 12th (10th: 10th: 10th: 8th) row to 65 (63: 63: 65: 57) sts, then on every foll - (12th: 12th: 12th: 10th) row until there are - (67: 69: 71: 73) sts, taking inc sts into st st.

Cont straight until sleeve measures 45 (45: 46: 46: 46) cm, ending with a WS row.

Shape top

Keeping patt correct, cast off 5 (6: 6: 7: 7) sts at beg of next 2 rows. 55 (55: 57: 57: 59) sts.

Dec 1 st at each end of next 5 rows, then on foll 2 alt rows, then on every foll 4th row until 33 (33: 35: 35: 37) sts rem.

Work 1 row, ending with a WS row.

Dec 1 st at each end of next and every foll alt row to 25 sts, then on foll 3 rows, ending with a WS row.

Cast off rem 19 sts.

MAKING UP

PRESS as described on the information page.

Join both shoulder seams using back stitch, or mattress stitch if preferred.

Button band

Cast on 7 sts using 3¼ mm (US 3) needles and yarn B.

Break off yarn B and join in yarn A.

Row 1 (RS): K2, P1, K1, P1, K2.

Row 2: K1, (P1, K1) 3 times.

These 2 rows form rib.

Cont in rib until button band, when slightly stretched, fits up left front opening edge from cast-on edge to neck shaping, ending with a WS row.

Break yarn and leave sts on a holder.

Slip st band in place.

Mark positions for 7 buttons on this band – first to come 2.5 cm up from cast-on edge, last to come just above neck shaping, and rem 5 buttons evenly spaced between.

Buttonhole band

Cast on 7 sts using 3¼ mm (US 3) needles and yarn B.

Break off yarn B and join in yarn A.

Cont in rib as given for button band until buttonhole band, when slightly stretched, fits up right front opening edge from cast-on edge to neck shaping, ending with a WS row and working 6 buttonholes to correspond with positions marked for buttons on left front as folls:

Buttonhole row (RS): K2, P2tog, yrn, P1, K2.

When band is complete, do NOT break yarn.

Slip st band in place.

Neckband

With RS facing, using 3¼ mm (US 3) needles and yarn A, rib across 7 sts of buttonhole band, pick up and knit 26 (27: 27: 29: 29) sts up right side of neck, 31 (33: 33: 35: 35) sts from back,

and 26 (27: 27: 29: 29) sts down left side of neck, then rib across 7 sts of button band. 97 (101: 101: 107: 107) sts.

Cont in rib as set by bands for 1 row.

Row 2 (RS): K2, P2tog, yrn, rib to end.

Work in rib for a further 3 rows.

Cast off in rib.

Embroidery

Following diagram, embroider flowers, stems and leaves onto fronts and sleeves.

See information page for finishing instructions, setting in sleeves using the set-in method.

French Knot

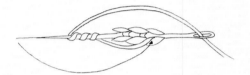

Laisy Daisy

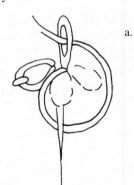

a.

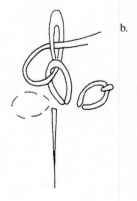

b.

Embroidery Diagram

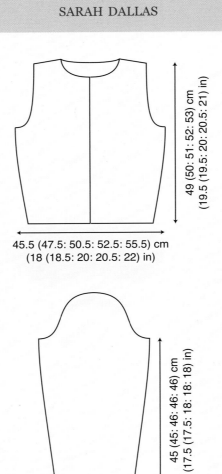

49 (50: 51: 52: 53) cm
(19.5 (19.5: 20: 20.5: 21) in)

45.5 (47.5: 50.5: 52.5: 55.5) cm
(18 (18.5: 20: 20.5: 22) in)

45 (45: 46: 46: 46) cm
(17.5 (17.5: 18: 18: 18) in)

FAYE

KIM HARGREAVES

More of a wrap than a cardigan, this design works a treat slipped over a period floral
dress to keep out the chill autumn air. The simple, soft shape makes it ideal to wear for a
dinner party, especially with a patterned dress, as in our picture.

FAYE

KIM HARGREAVES

YARN

	XS	S	M	L	XL	
To fit bust	81	86	91	97	102	cm
	32	34	36	38	40	in

Rowan Kid Silk Haze

| | 8 | 8 | 8 | 9 | 9 | x 25gm |

(photographed in Trance 582)

NEEDLES

1 pair 3¼ mm (no 10) (US 3) needles

1 pair 3¾ mm (no 9) (US 5) needles

2 double-pointed 2¾ mm (no 12)
(US 2) needles

TENSION

22 sts and 32 rows to 10 cm measured over pattern using 3¾ mm (US 5) needles and yarn DOUBLE.

BACK

Cast on 95 (101: 107: 113: 119) sts using 3¼ mm (US 3) needles and yarn DOUBLE.

Row 1 (RS): K1, *P1, K1, rep from * to end.

Row 2: P1, *K1, P1, rep from * to end.

These 2 rows form rib.

Cont in rib for 12 cm, ending with a WS row.

Next row (eyelet row) (RS): Rib 2 (5: 2: 5: 2), *yrn, work 2 tog, rib 4, rep from * to last 3 (6: 3: 6: 3) sts, yrn, work 2 tog, rib 1 (4: 1: 4: 1).

Cont in rib for a further 3 rows, inc 1 st at end of last row and ending with a WS row.

96 (102: 108: 114: 120) sts.

Change to 3¾ mm (US 5) needles.

Row 1 (RS): K0 (1: 0: 1: 0), *K2, yfwd, sl 1, K1, psso, rep from * to last 0 (1: 0: 1: 0) st, K0 (1: 0: 1: 0).

Row 2: P0 (1: 0: 1: 0), *P2, yrn, P2tog, rep from * to last 0 (1: 0: 1: 0) st, P0 (1: 0: 1: 0).

These 2 rows form patt.

Cont in patt until back measures 37 (38: 38: 39: 39) cm, ending with a WS row.

Shape armholes

Keeping patt correct, cast off 3 (4: 4: 5: 5) sts at beg of next 2 rows.

90 (94: 100: 104: 110) sts.

Dec 1 st at each end of next 5 (5: 7: 7: 9) rows, then on foll 2 (3: 3: 4: 4) alt rows.

76 (78: 80: 82: 84) sts.

Cont straight until armhole measures 20 (20: 21: 21: 22) cm, ending with a WS row.

Shape shoulders and back neck

Cast off 7 (7: 8: 8: 8) sts at beg of next 2 rows.

62 (64: 64: 66: 68) sts.

Next row (RS): Cast off 7 (7: 8: 8: 8) sts, patt until there are 12 (12: 11: 11: 12) sts on right needle and turn, leaving rem sts on a holder. Work each side of neck separately.

Cast off 4 sts at beg of next row.

Cast off rem 8 (8: 7: 7: 8) sts.

With RS facing, rejoin yarn to rem sts, cast off centre 24 (26: 26: 28: 28) sts, patt to end.

Complete to match first side, reversing shapings.

LEFT FRONT

Cast on 52 (56: 58: 62: 64) sts using 3¼ mm (US 3) needles and yarn DOUBLE.

Row 1 (RS): *K1, P1, rep from * to last 2 sts, K2.

Row 2: *K1, P1, rep from * to end.

These 2 rows form rib.

Cont in rib for 12 cm, ending with a WS row.

Next row (eyelet row) (RS): Rib 5 (2: 5: 2: 5), *yrn, work 2 tog, rib 4, rep from * to last 5 (6: 5: 6: 5) sts, yrn, work 2 tog, rib 3 (4: 3: 4: 3).

Cont in rib for a further 2 rows, ending with a RS row.

Next row (WS): Rib 5 and slip these 5 sts onto a holder, rib to last 1 (0: 1: 0: 1) st, (inc in last st) 1 (0: 1: 0: 1) times. 48 (51: 54: 57: 60) sts.

Change to 3¾ mm (US 5) needles.

Row 1 (RS): K0 (1: 0: 1: 0), *K2, yfwd, sl 1, K1, psso, rep from * to last 0 (2: 2: 0: 0) sts, K0 (2: 2: 0: 0).

Row 2: P0 (2: 2: 0: 0), *P2, yrn, P2tog, rep from * to last 0 (1: 0: 1: 0) st, P0 (1: 0: 1: 0).

These 2 rows form patt.

Work in patt for a further 6 rows, ending with a WS row.

Shape front slope

Keeping patt correct, dec 1 st at end of next and every foll 8th row until left front matches back to beg of armhole shaping, ending with a WS row.

Shape armhole

Keeping patt correct and still dec 1 st at front slope edge on every 8th row as set **throughout**, cont as folls:

Cast off 3 (4: 4: 5: 5) sts at beg of next row.

Work 1 row.

Dec 1 st at armhole edge of next 5 (5: 7: 7: 9) rows, then on foll 2 (3: 3: 4: 4) alt rows.

Cont to dec at front slope edge on every 8th row as set until 22 (22: 23: 23: 24) sts rem.

Cont straight until left front matches back to start of shoulder shaping, ending with a WS row.

Shape shoulder

Cast off 7 (7: 8: 8: 8) sts at beg of next and foll alt row.

Work 1 row.

Cast off rem 8 (8: 7: 7: 8) sts.

RIGHT FRONT

Cast on 52 (56: 58: 62: 64) sts using 3¼ mm (US 3) needles and yarn DOUBLE.

Row 1 (RS): K2, *P1, K1, rep from * to end.

Row 2: *P1, K1, rep from * to end.

These 2 rows form rib.

Cont in rib for 12 cm, ending with a WS row.

Next row (eyelet row) (RS): Rib 3 (4: 3: 4: 3), work 2 tog tbl, yrn, *rib 4, work 2 tog tbl, yrn, rep from * to last 5 (2: 5: 2: 5) sts, rib 5 (2: 5: 2: 5).

Cont in rib for a further 2 rows, ending with a RS row.

Next row (WS): (Inc in first st) 1 (0: 1: 0: 1) times, rib to last 5 sts and turn, leaving last 5 sts on a holder.

48 (51: 54: 57: 60) sts.

Change to 3³/₄ mm (US 5) needles.

Row 1 (RS): K0 (2: 2: 0: 0), *K2, yfwd, sl 1, K1, psso, rep from * to last 0 (1: 0: 1: 0) st, K0 (1: 0: 1: 0).

Row 2: P0 (1: 0: 1: 0), *P2, yrn, P2tog, rep from * to last 0 (2: 2: 0: 0) sts, P0 (2: 0: 1: 0).

These 2 rows form patt.

Work in patt for a further 6 rows, ending with a WS row.

Shape front slope

Keeping patt correct, dec 1 st at beg of next and every foll 8th row until left front matches back to beg of armhole shaping, ending with a RS row.

Complete to match left front, reversing shapings.

SLEEVES (both alike)

Cast on 57 (57: 59: 61: 61) sts using 3¹/₄ mm (US 3) needles and yarn DOUBLE.

Work in rib as given for back for 7 cm, inc 1 st at end of last row and ending with a WS row.
58 (58: 60: 62: 62) sts.

Change to 3³/₄ mm (US 5) needles.

Row 1 (RS): K1 (1: 0: 1: 1), *K2, yfwd, sl 1, K1, psso, rep from * to last 1 (1: 0: 1: 1) st, K1 (1: 0: 1: 1).

Row 2: P1 (1: 0: 1: 1), *P2, yrn, P2tog, rep from * to last 1 (1: 0: 1: 1) st, P1 (1: 0: 1: 1).

These 2 rows form patt.

Cont in patt, shaping sides by inc 1 st at each end of 17th (13th: 13th: 13th: 11th) and every foll 20th (16th: 16th: 16th: 14th) row to 68 (66: 66: 68: 72) sts, then on every foll - (18th: 18th: 18th: 16th) row until there are - (70: 72: 74: 76) sts, taking inc sts into patt.

Cont straight until sleeve measures 43 (43: 44: 44: 44) cm, ending with a WS row.

Shape top

Keeping patt correct, cast off 3 (4: 4: 5: 5) sts at beg of next 2 rows.
62 (62: 64: 64: 66) sts.

Dec 1 st at each end of next 3 rows, then on

foll 2 alt rows, then on every foll 4th row until 40 (40: 42: 42: 44) sts rem.

Work 1 row, ending with a WS row.

Dec 1 st at each end of next and every foll alt row to 36 sts, then on foll 7 rows, ending with a WS row.

Cast off rem 22 sts.

MAKING UP

PRESS as described on the information page.

Join both shoulder seams using back stitch, or mattress stitch if preferred.

Left front band

Slip 5 sts from holder onto 3¹/₄ mm (US 3) needles and rejoin yarn DOUBLE with RS facing.

Cont in rib as set until band, when slightly stretched, fits up left front opening edge and across to centre back neck.

Cast off.

Slip stitch band in place.

Right front band

Slip 5 sts from holder onto 3¹/₄ mm (US 3) needles and rejoin yarn DOUBLE with WS facing.

Cont in rib as set until band, when slightly stretched, fits up right front opening edge and across to centre back neck.

Cast off.

Slip stitch band in place, joining ends of bands at centre back neck.

Tie

With double-pointed 2³/₄ mm (US 2) needles and yarn SINGLE, cast on 4 sts.

Row 1 (RS): K4, *without turning work slip these 4 sts to opposite end of needle and bring yarn to opposite end of work pulling it quite tightly across back of these 4 sts, using other needle K these 4 sts again; rep from * until tie is 130 cm long, K4tog and fasten off.

See information page for finishing instructions, setting in sleeves using the set-in method.

Thread tie through eyelet row near top of ribbing.

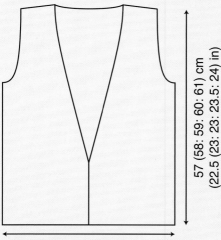

43.5 (46.5: 49: 52: 54.5) cm
(17 (18.5: 19.5: 20.5: 21.5) in)

57 (58: 59: 60: 61) cm
(22.5 (23: 23: 23.5: 24) in)

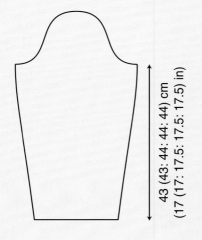

43 (43: 44: 44: 44) cm
(17 (17: 17.5: 17.5: 17.5) in)

MASON
KIM HARGREAVES

Rugged enough to look at home on an *ouvrier* pruning the winter vines or *pecheur* out on his fishing boat, the dark hints of colour in this roll neck supply subtle visual interest. The cabling hints at ropes and twine.

MASON
KIM HARGREAVES

YARN

	S	M	L	XL	XXL	
To fit chest	97	102	107	112	117	cm
	38	40	42	44	46	in

Rowan Yorkshire Tweed Chunky

| | 9 | 10 | 10 | 10 | 11 | x100gm |

(photographed in Rivet 552)

NEEDLES

1 pair 7mm (no 2) (US 10½) needles
1 pair 8mm (no 0) (US 11) needles
Cable needle

TENSION

12 sts and 16 rows to 10 cm measured over
stocking stitch using 8mm (US 11) needles.

SPECIAL ABBREVIATIONS

C10B = slip next 5 sts onto cable needle and
leave at back of work, K5, then K5 from cable
needle.

C10F = slip next 5 sts onto cable needle and
leave at front of work, K5, then K5 from cable
needle.

BACK

Cast on 74 (76: 80: 82: 86) sts using 7mm
(US 10½) needles.
Row 1 (RS): K0 (0: 1: 0: 0), P0 (1: 2: 0: 2),
*K2, P2, rep from * to last 2 (3: 1: 2: 0) sts,
K2 (2: 1: 2: 0), P0 (1: 0: 0: 0).
Row 2: P0 (0: 1: 0: 0), K0 (1: 2: 0: 2), *P2, K2,
rep from * to last 2 (3: 1: 2: 0) sts,
P2 (2: 1: 2: 0), K0 (1: 0: 0: 0).
These 2 rows form rib.
Cont in rib for a further 12 rows, ending with a
WS row.
Change to 8mm (US 11) needles.
Row 1 (RS): P12 (13: 15: 16: 18), K10, P30,
K10, P to end.
Row 2 and every foll alt row: K12 (13: 15:
16: 18), P10, K30, P10, K to end.
Rows 3, 5 and 7: As row 1.

Row 9: P12 (13: 15: 16: 18), C10B, P30,
C10F, P to end.
Row 11: As row 1.
Row 12: As row 2.
These 12 rows form patt.
Cont in patt until back measures 43 (43: 44:
44: 45) cm, ending with a WS row.
Shape armholes
Keeping patt correct, cast off 4 sts at beg of
next 2 rows.
66 (68: 72: 74: 78) sts.
Dec 1 st at each end of next 3 (3: 5: 5: 7) rows,
then on foll 3 alt rows.
54 (56: 56: 58: 58) sts.
Cont straight until armhole measures 22 (23:
23: 24: 24) cm, ending with a WS row.
Shape shoulders and back neck
Cast off 5 sts at beg of next 2 rows.
44 (46: 46: 48: 48) sts.
Next row (RS): Cast off 5 sts, patt until there
are 9 sts on right needle and turn, leaving rem
sts on a holder.
Work each side of neck separately.
Cast off 4 sts at beg of next row.
Cast off rem 5 sts.
With RS facing, rejoin yarn to rem sts, cast off
centre 16 (18: 18: 20: 20) sts, patt to end.
Complete to match first side, reversing
shapings.

FRONT

Work as given for back until 10 (10: 12:
12: 12) rows less have been worked than on
back to start of shoulder shaping, ending
with a WS row.
Shape neck
Next row (RS): Patt 22 (22: 23: 23: 23) sts and
turn, leaving rem sts on a holder.
Work each side of neck separately.
Dec 1 st at neck edge of next 6 rows, then on
foll 1 (1: 2: 2: 2) alt rows.
15 sts.
Work 1 row, ending with a WS row.

Shape shoulder
Cast off 5 sts at beg of next and foll alt row.
Work 1 row.
Cast off rem 5 sts.
With RS facing, rejoin yarn to rem sts,
cast off centre 10 (12: 10: 12: 12) sts,
patt to end.
Complete to match first side, reversing
shapings.

LEFT SLEEVE

Cast on 40 (40: 40: 42: 42) sts using 7mm
(US 10½) needles.
Row 1 (RS): K1 (1: 1: 2: 2), P2, *K2, P2, rep
from * to last 1 (1: 1: 2: 2) sts, K1 (1: 1: 2: 2).
Row 2: P1 (1: 1: 2: 2), K2, *P2, K2, rep from
* to last 1 (1: 1: 2: 2) sts, P1 (1: 1: 2: 2).
These 2 rows form rib.
Cont in rib for a further 14 rows, ending with a
WS row.
Change to 8mm (US 11) needles.
Row 1 (RS): Inc in first st, P14 (14: 14: 15:
15), K10, P to last st, inc in last st.
42 (42: 42: 44: 44) sts.
Row 2: K16 (16: 16: 17: 17), P10, K to end.
Row 3: P16 (16: 16: 17: 17), K10, P to end.
Rows 4 to 7: As rows 2 and 3, twice.
Row 8: As row 3.
Row 9: Inc in first st, P15 (15: 15: 16: 16),
C10F, P to last st, inc in last st.
44 (44: 44: 46: 46) sts.
Row 10: K17 (17: 17: 18: 18), P10, K to end.
Row 11: P17 (17: 17: 18: 18), K10, P to end.
Row 12: As row 10.
These 12 rows form patt and start sleeve
shaping.
Cont in patt, shaping sides by inc 1 st at each
end of 5th and every foll 8th row to 48 (56: 56:
56: 56) sts, then on every foll 10th (-: -: 10th:
10th) row until there are 54 (-: -: 58: 58) sts,
taking inc sts into rev st st.
Cont straight until sleeve measures 49 (50: 50:
51: 51) cm, ending with a WS row.

Shape top

Keeping patt correct, cast off 4 sts at beg of next 2 rows.

46 (48: 48: 50: 50) sts.

Dec 1 st at each end of next 3 rows, then on foll alt row, then on every foll 4th row until 32 (34: 34: 36: 36) sts rem.

Work 1 row, ending with a WS row.

Dec 1 st at each end of next and foll 0 (1: 1: 2: 2) alt rows, then on foll 3 rows, ending with a WS row.

Cast off rem 24 sts.

RIGHT SLEEVE

Work as given for left sleeve, replacing "C10F" of patt with "C10B".

MAKING UP

PRESS as described on the information page. Join right shoulder seam using back stitch, or mattress stitch if preferred.

Collar

With RS facing and using 7mm (US 10½) needles, pick up and knit 14 (14: 15: 15: 15) sts down left side of neck, 10 (12: 10: 12: 12) sts from front, 14 (14: 15: 15: 15) sts up right side of neck, then 24 (26: 26: 28: 28) sts from back. 62 (66: 66: 70: 70) sts.

Row 1 (WS): P2, *K2, P2, rep from * to end.

Row 2: K2, *P2, K2, rep from * to end.

These 2 rows form rib.

Cont in rib until collar measures 8 cm.

Change to 8mm (US 11) needles.

Cont in rib until collar measures 20 cm.

Cast off in rib.

See information page for finishing instructions, setting in sleeves using the set-in method.

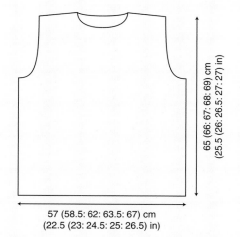

57 (58.5: 62: 63.5: 67) cm
(22.5 (23: 24.5: 25: 26.5) in)

65 (66: 67: 68: 69) cm
(25.5 (26: 26.5: 27: 27) in)

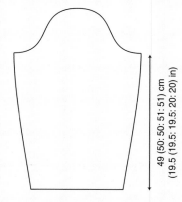

49 (50: 50: 51: 51) cm
(19.5 (19.5: 19.5: 20: 20) in)

JOLIE
KIM HARGREAVES

There's a touch of homespun quaintness about this low fastening cardigan, which enhances a curvy figure. The nubbly surface, seen here in a neutral colour, reflects the natural slightly uneven materials of the village street: the crumbly plaster, the distressed shutters, the cobbles underfoot.

JOLIE
KIM HARGREAVES

YARN

	XS	S	M	L	XL	
To fit bust	81	86	91	97	102	cm
	32	34	36	38	40	in

Rowan Yorkshire Tweed Aran

| | 5 | 5 | 6 | 6 | 7 | x100gm |

(photographed in Tusk 417)

NEEDLES

1 pair 5mm (no 6) (US 8) needles

CROCHET HOOK

6.00mm (no 4) (US J10) crochet hook

BUTTONS – 9 x 00339

TENSION

17 ½ sts and 29 rows to 10 cm measured over pattern using 5mm (US 8) needles.

BACK

Left side panel

Cast on 24 (26: 28: 30: 32) sts using 5mm (US 8) needles.

Starting and ending rows as indicated, working chart rows 1 to 18 **7 times in total,** then working chart rows 19 to 24 **once only** and then repeating chart rows 25 to 38 throughout, cont in patt from chart for body as folls:

Dec 1 st at end of 15th and every foll 6th row to 21 (23: 25: 27: 29) sts, then on every foll 4th row until 19 (21: 23: 25: 27) sts rem.

Work 1 row, ending with a WS row.

Break yarn and leave sts on a holder.

Centre panel

Cast on 35 sts using 5mm (US 8) needles.

Starting and ending rows as indicated, cont in patt from chart for body as folls:

Work 36 rows, ending with a WS row.

Break yarn and leave sts on a holder.

Right side panel

Cast on 24 (26: 28: 30: 32) sts using 5mm (US 8) needles.

Starting and ending rows as indicated, cont in patt from chart for body as folls:

Dec 1 st at beg of 15th and every foll 6th row to 21 (23: 25: 27: 29) sts, then on every foll 4th row until 19 (21: 23: 25: 27) sts rem.

Work 1 row, ending with a WS row.

Join panels

Next row (RS): Patt to last 4 sts of right side panel, holding WS of centre panel against RS of right side panel, patt tog first st of centre panel with next st of right side panel, patt tog next 3 sts of centre panel with rem 3 sts of right side panel in same way, patt to last 4 sts of centre panel, holding WS of centre panel against RS of left side panel, patt tog next st of centre panel with first st of left side panel, patt tog last 3 sts of centre panel with next 3 sts of

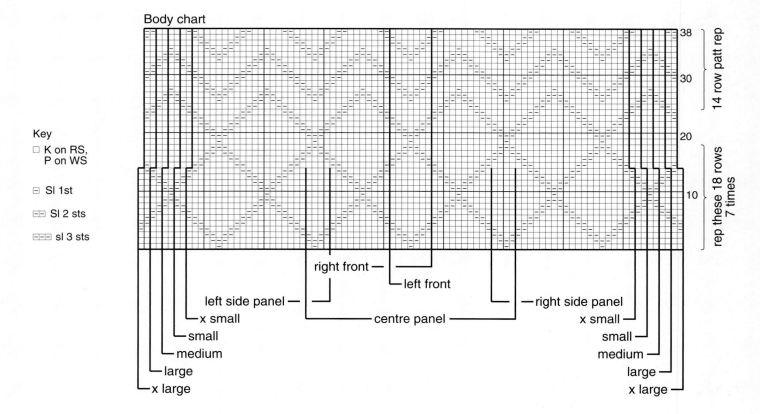

Body chart

Key
□ K on RS, P on WS

⊟ Sl 1st

⊟⊟ Sl 2 sts

⊟⊟⊟ sl 3 sts

38
30
20
10

14 row patt rep

rep these 18 rows 7 times

right front —
left front —
left side panel —
centre panel —
right side panel —
x small
small
medium
large
x large
x small
small
medium
large
x large

left side panel in same way, patt to end.
65 (69: 73: 77: 81) sts.

Work 1 row.

Dec 1 st at each end of next row.
63 (67: 71: 75: 79) sts.

Cont straight until back measures 16 (17: 17: 18: 18) cm, ending with a WS row.

Inc 1 st at each end of next and every foll 8th row until there are 75 (79: 83: 87: 91) sts, taking inc sts into patt.

Work 13 rows, ending with a WS row. (Back should measure 35 (36: 36: 37: 37) cm.)

Shape armholes

Keeping patt correct, cast off 3 (4: 4: 5: 5) sts at beg of next 2 rows. 69 (71: 75: 77: 81) sts.

Dec 1 st at each end of next 3 rows, then on foll 3 (3: 4: 4: 5) alt rows. 57 (59: 61: 63: 65) sts.

Cont straight until armhole measures 20 (20: 21: 21: 22) cm, ending with a WS row.

Shape shoulders and back neck

Cast off 5 (5: 6: 6: 6) sts at beg of next 2 rows. 47 (49: 49: 51: 53) sts.

Next row (RS): Cast off 5 (5: 6: 6: 6) sts, patt until there are 10 (10: 9: 9: 10) sts on right needle and turn, leaving rem sts on a holder.

Work each side of neck separately.

Cast off 4 sts at beg of next row.

Cast off rem 6 (6: 5: 5: 6) sts.

With RS facing, rejoin yarn to rem sts, cast off centre 17 (19: 19: 21: 21) sts, patt to end.

Complete to match first side, reversing shapings.

LEFT FRONT

Cast on 41 (43: 45: 47: 49) sts using 5mm (US 8) needles.

Starting and ending rows as indicated, cont in patt from chart for body as folls:

Dec 1 st at beg of 15th and every foll 6th row to 38 (40: 42: 44: 46) sts, then on every foll 4th row until 35 (37: 39: 41: 43) sts rem.

Cont straight until left front measures 16 (17: 17: 18: 18) cm, ending with a WS row.

Inc 1 st at beg of next row. 36 (38: 40: 42: 44) sts.

Work 7 rows, ending with a WS row.

Shape front slope

Inc 1 st at side seam edge (beg) of next and 4 foll 8th rows **and at same time** dec 1 st at front slope edge (end) of next and 5 foll 4th rows, then on every foll 6th row.

33 (35: 37: 39: 41) sts.

Dec 1 st at front slope edge **only** of 6th and foll 0 (6th: 6th: 6th: 6th) row. 32 (33: 35: 37: 39) sts.

Work 7 (1: 1: 1: 1) rows, ending with a WS row. (Left front now matches back to beg of armhole shaping.)

Shape armholes

Keeping patt correct, cast off 3 (4: 4: 5: 5) sts at beg and dec 1 (0: 0: 0: 0) st at end of next row.
28 (29: 31: 32: 34) sts.

Work 1 row.

Dec 1 st at armhole edge of next 3 rows, then on foll 3 (3: 4: 4: 5) alt rows **and at same time** dec 1 st at front slope edge of 7th (3rd: 3rd: 3rd: 3rd) and foll 0 (6th: 6th: 6th: 6th) row.
21 (21: 22: 23: 24) sts.

Dec 1 st at front slope edge **only** on 6th (6th: 6th: 4th: 2nd) and every foll 8th (8th: 8th: 6th: 6th) to 16 (16: 17: 19: 22) sts, then on every foll - (-: -: 8th: 8th) until - (-: -: 17: 18) sts rem.

Cont straight until left front matches back to start of shoulder shaping, ending with a WS row.

Shape shoulder

Cast off 5 (5: 6: 6: 6) sts at beg of next and foll alt row.

Work 1 row.

Cast off rem 6 (6: 5: 5: 6) sts.

Mark positions for 3 buttons along left front opening edge – first to come level with row 37, third to come just below start of front slope shaping, and second to come midway between.

RIGHT FRONT

Cast on 41 (43: 45: 47: 49) sts using 5mm (US 8) needles.

Starting and ending rows as indicated, cont in patt from chart for body as folls:

Dec 1 st at end of 15th and every foll 6th row to 38 (40: 42: 44: 46) sts, then on every foll 4th row until 36 (38: 40: 42: 44) sts rem.

Work 1 row, ending with a WS row.

Row 37 (buttonhole row) (RS): Patt 3 sts, cast off 2 sts (to make a buttonhole – cast on 2 sts over these cast-off sts on next row), patt to end.

Work 1 row.

Dec 1 st at end of next row. 35 (37: 39: 41: 43) sts.

Complete to match left front, reversing shapings and making a further 2 buttonholes to correspond with positions marked for buttons.

LEFT SLEEVE

Front panel

Cast on 31 (31: 31: 32: 32) sts using 5mm (US 8) needles.

Starting and ending rows as indicated, working chart rows 1 to 28 **once only,** and then repeating chart rows 29 to 46 throughout, cont in patt from chart for sleeve as folls:

Work 28 rows, ending with a WS row.

Break yarn and leave sts on a holder.

Back panel

Cast on 18 (18: 18: 19: 19) sts using 5mm (US 8) needles.

Starting and ending rows as indicated, cont in patt from chart for sleeve as folls:

Work 28 rows, ending with a WS row.

Join panels

Next row (RS): Patt to last 4 sts of back panel, holding WS of front panel against RS of back panel, patt tog first st of front panel with next st of back panel, patt tog next 3 sts of front panel with rem 3 sts of back panel in same way, patt to end. 45 (45: 45: 47: 47) sts.

**Work 1 row.

Inc 1 st at each end of next and every foll 20th (16th: 14th: 14th: 12th) row until there are 55 (57: 59: 61: 63) sts, taking inc sts into patt.

Cont straight until sleeve measures 43 (43: 44: 44: 44) cm, ending with a WS row.

Shape top

Keeping patt correct, cast off 3 (4: 4: 5: 5) sts at beg of next 2 rows.

49 (49: 51: 51: 53) sts.

Dec 1 st at each end of next 3 rows, then on foll alt row, then on foll 4th row, then on every foll 6th row until 33 (33: 35: 35: 37) sts rem.

Work 3 rows, ending with a WS row.

Dec 1 st at each end of next and every foll alt row to 27 sts, then on foll 3 rows, ending with a WS row.

Cast off rem 21 sts.

RIGHT SLEEVE

Back panel

Cast on 18 (18: 18: 19: 19) sts using 5mm (US 8) needles.

Starting and ending rows as indicated, cont in patt from chart for sleeve as folls:

Work 28 rows, ending with a WS row.

Break yarn and leave sts on a holder.

Front panel

Cast on 31 (31: 31: 32: 32) sts using 5mm (US 8) needles.

Starting and ending rows as indicated, cont in patt from chart for sleeve as folls:

Work 28 rows, ending with a WS row.

Join panels

Next row (RS): Patt to last 4 sts of front panel, holding WS of front panel against RS of back panel, patt tog next st of front panel with first st of back panel, patt tog rem 3 sts of front panel with next 3 sts of back panel in same way, patt to end. 45 (45: 45: 47: 47) sts.

Complete as given for left sleeve from **.

MAKING UP

PRESS as described on the information page.

Join both shoulder seams using back stitch, or mattress stitch if preferred.

See information page for finishing instructions, setting in sleeves using the set-in method.

Edging

Using 6.00mm (US J10) crochet hook and starting at point where right back panel joins centre panel, work 1 row of double crochet evenly down right back panel row-end edge, across cast-on edge to front opening edge, up front opening edge and front slope, across back neck, down left front slope and opening edge, across cast-on edge to back vent, then up row-end edge of left back panel to point where left back panel joins centre panel, working 2 dc into corners and ensuring edging lays flat, do NOT turn.

Now work 1 row of crab st (double crochet worked from left to right, instead of right to left).

Fasten off.

In same way, work edging along row-end and cast-on edges of back centre panel, then along sleeve cast-on and row-end edges of panels.

Using photograph as a guide, attach 3 buttons to each cuff, attaching buttons through both layers.

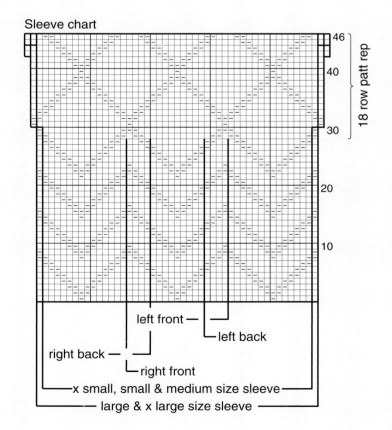

Sleeve chart

18 row patt rep

left front

left back

right back

right front

x small, small & medium size sleeve

large & x large size sleeve

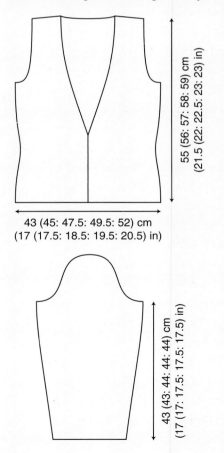

43 (45: 47.5: 49.5: 52) cm
(17 (17.5: 18.5: 19.5: 20.5) in)

55 (56: 57: 58: 59) cm
(21.5 (22: 22.5: 23: 23) in)

43 (43: 44: 44: 44) cm
(17 (17: 17.5: 17.5: 17.5) in)

The unusual vertical stripes and daring colour combination give this design an artistic style. The striped jacket and floral pattern on the dress co-ordinate with each other, bringing to mind avant-garde French artists who looked to the Far East for their inspiration.

YARN

	XS	S	M	L	XL	
To fit bust	81	86	91	97	102	cm
	32	34	36	38	40	in

Rowan Yorkshire Tweed 4 ply

A Stainless 270						
	5	5	5	5	5	x 25gm
B Foxy 275						
	3	3	3	4	4	x 25gm
C Radiant 276						
	4	4	4	4	4	x 25gm
D Brilliant 274						
	3	4	4	4	4	x 25gm

NEEDLES

1 pair 2³/₄ mm (no 12) (US 2) needles
1 pair 3¹/₄ mm (no 10) (US 3) needles

TENSION

25 sts and 38 rows to 10 cm measured over pattern using 3¹/₄ mm (US 3) needles.

BACK

Cast on 110 (116: 122: 128: 134) sts using 2³/₄ mm (US 2) needles and yarn A.
Work in garter st for 4 rows, end with a WS row.
Change to 3¹/₄ mm (US 3) needles.
Starting and ending rows as indicated, using the **intarsia** technique as described on the information page, working chart rows 1 and 2 **once only** and then repeating chart rows 3 to 10 throughout, cont in patt from chart for body as folls:
Dec 1 st at each end of 17th and every foll 10th row until 100 (106: 112: 118: 124) sts rem.
Work 33 rows, ending with a WS row.

Inc 1 st at each end of next and every foll 10th row until there are 110 (116: 122: 128: 134) sts, taking inc sts into patt.
Cont straight until back measures 39 (40: 40: 41: 41) cm, ending with a WS row.

Shape armholes

Keeping patt correct, cast off 4 (5: 5: 6: 6) sts at beg of next 2 rows, then 3 sts at beg of foll 2 rows.
96 (100: 106: 110: 116) sts.
Dec 1 st at each end of next 3 (3: 5: 5: 7) rows, then on foll 1 (2: 2: 3: 3) alt rows, then on every foll 4th row until 84 (86: 88: 90: 92) sts rem.
Cont straight until armhole measures 18 (18: 19: 19: 20) cm, ending with a WS row.

Shape shoulders and back neck

Cast off 8 (8: 9: 9: 9) sts at beg of next 2 rows.
68 (70: 70: 72: 74) sts.

Next row (RS): Cast off 8 (8: 9: 9: 9) sts, patt until there are 13 (13: 12: 12: 13) sts on right needle and turn, leaving rem sts on a holder.
Work each side of neck separately.
Cast off 4 sts at beg of next row.
Cast off rem 9 (9: 8: 8: 9) sts.
With RS facing, rejoin yarns to rem sts, cast off centre 26 (28: 28: 30: 30) sts, patt to end.
Complete to match first side, reversing shapings.

LEFT FRONT

Cast on 58 (61: 64: 67: 70) sts using 2³/₄ mm (US 2) needles and yarn A.
Work in garter st for 4 rows, ending with a WS row.
Change to 3¹/₄ mm (US 3) needles.
Starting and ending rows as indicated, cont in patt from chart for body as folls:

Row 1 (RS): Work first 55 (58: 61: 64: 67) sts as row 1 of chart, using yarn A K3.

Row 2: Using yarn A K3, work last 55 (58: 61: 64: 67) sts as row 2 of chart.

These 2 rows set the sts – front opening edge 3 sts in garter st using yarn A and all other sts in patt from chart.
Keeping sts correct as now set throughout, dec 1 st at beg of 15th and every foll 10th row until 53 (56: 59: 62: 65) sts rem.
Work 33 rows, ending with a WS row.
Inc 1 st at beg of next and every foll 10th row until there are 58 (61: 64: 67: 70) sts, taking inc sts into patt.
Cont straight until left front matches back to beg of armhole shaping, ending with a WS row.

Shape armhole

Keeping patt correct, cast off 4 (5: 5: 6: 6) sts at beg of next row, then 3 sts at beg of foll alt row.
51 (53: 56: 58: 61) sts.
Work 1 row.
Dec 1 st at armhole edge of next 3 (3: 5: 5: 7) rows, then on foll 1 (2: 2: 3: 3) alt rows, then on every foll 4th row until 45 (46: 47: 48: 49) sts rem.
Cont straight until 15 (15: 15: 17: 17) rows less have been worked than on back to start of shoulder shaping, ending with a RS row.

Shape neck

Next row (WS): Patt 11 (12: 12: 12: 12) sts and slip these sts onto a holder, patt to end.
34 (34: 35: 36: 37) sts.
Keeping patt correct, work 1 row.
Cast off 4 sts at beg of next row.
30 (30: 31: 32: 33) sts.

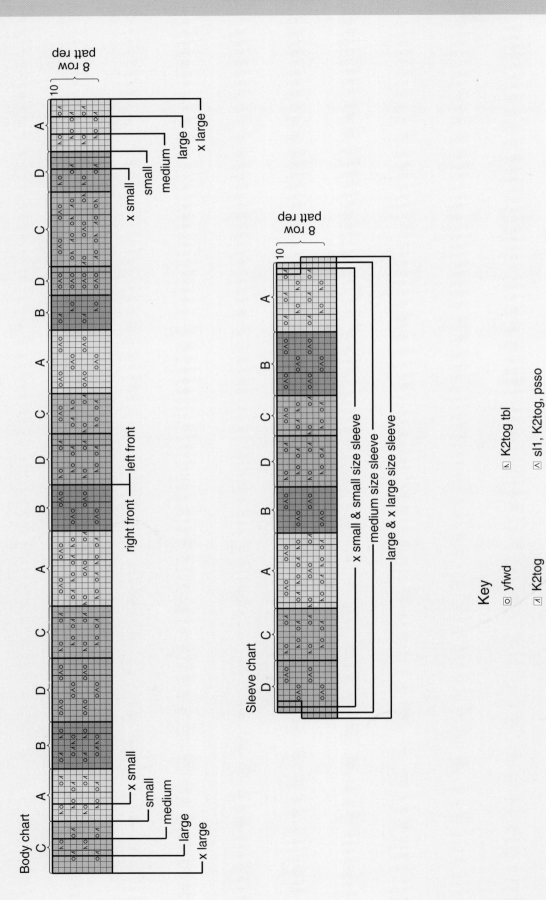

Body chart

Sleeve chart

8 row patt rep

10

x small
small
medium
large
x large

right front — left front

Key

⊙ yfwd

↘ K2tog

↘ K2tog tbl

↙ sl1, K2tog, psso

x small & small size sleeve

medium size sleeve

large & x large size sleeve

Dec 1 st at neck edge of next 3 rows, then on foll 2 (2: 2: 3: 3) alt rows. 25 (25: 26: 26: 27) sts. Work 5 rows, ending with a WS row.

Shape shoulder

Cast off 8 (8: 9: 9: 9) sts at beg of next and foll alt row.

Work 1 row.

Cast off rem 9 (9: 8: 8: 9) sts.

RIGHT FRONT

Cast on 58 (61: 64: 67: 70) sts using 2³/4 mm (US 2) needles and yarn A.

Work in garter st for 4 rows, ending with a WS row.

Change to 3¹/4 mm (US 3) needles.

Starting and ending rows as indicated, cont in patt from chart for body as folls:

Row 1 (RS): Using yarn A K3, work last 55 (58: 61: 64: 67) sts as row 1 of chart.

Row 2: Work first 55 (58: 61: 64: 67) sts as row 2 of chart, using yarn A K3.

These 2 rows set the sts – front opening edge 3 sts in garter st using yarn A and all other sts in patt from chart.

Keeping sts correct as now set throughout, complete to match left front, reversing shapings.

SLEEVES (both alike)

Cast on 76 (76: 78: 80: 80) sts using 2³/4 mm (US 2) needles and yarn A.

Work in garter st for 4 rows, end with a WS row.

Change to 3¹/4 mm (US 3) needles.

Starting and ending rows as indicated, using the **intarsia** technique as described on the information page, working chart rows 1 and 2 **once only** and then repeating chart rows 3 to 10 throughout, cont in patt from chart for sleeve as folls:

Dec 1 st at each end of 7th and every foll 10th row until 66 (66: 68: 70: 70) sts rem.

Work 49 rows, ending with a WS row.

Inc 1 st at each end of next and every foll 10th (8th: 8th: 8th: 6th) row to 72 (72: 80: 82: 84) sts, then on every foll 12th (10th: 10th: 10th: 8th) row until there are 78 (80: 84: 86: 90) sts, taking inc sts into patt.

Cont straight until sleeve measures 46 (46: 47: 47: 47) cm, ending with a WS row.

Shape top

Keeping patt correct, cast off 4 (5: 5: 6: 6) sts at beg of next 2 rows, then 3 sts at beg of foll 2 rows.

64 (64: 68: 68: 72) sts.

Dec 1 st at each end of next 3 rows, then on foll 4 alt rows, then on every foll 4th row until 40 (40: 44: 44: 48) sts rem.

Work 1 row, ending with a WS row.

Dec 1 st at each end of next and every foll alt row to 30 sts, then on foll 2 rows, ending with a RS row. 26 sts.

Cast off 3 sts at beg of next 4 rows.

Cast off rem 14 sts.

MAKING UP

PRESS as described on the information page.

Join both shoulder seams using back stitch, or mattress stitch if preferred.

Neckband

With RS facing, using 2 3/4mm (US 2) needles and yarn A, slip 11 (12: 12: 12: 12) sts from right front holder onto right needle, rejoin yarn and pick up and knit 18 (18: 18: 20: 20) sts up right side of neck, 34 (36: 36: 38: 38) sts from back, and 18 (18: 18: 20: 20) sts down left side of neck, then knit across 11 (12: 12: 12: 12) sts left on left front holder.

92 (96: 96: 102: 102) sts.

Work in garter st for 2 rows.

Cast off knitwise (on WS).

See information page for finishing instructions, setting in sleeves using the set-in method.

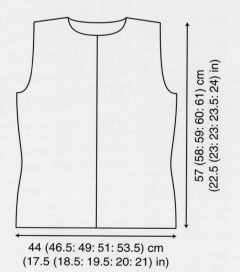

44 (46.5: 49: 51: 53.5) cm
(17.5 (18.5: 19.5: 20: 21) in)

57 (58: 59: 60: 61) cm
(22.5 (23: 23: 23.5: 24) in)

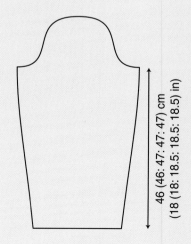

46 (46: 47: 47: 47) cm
(18 (18: 18.5: 18.5: 18.5) in)

CHANTEL
KIM HARGREAVES

This crocheted shawl is a true labour of love: once made, it will be treasured for always.
The repeated gem-like motif plays with shape and colour. Worn here with a slim, pink
dress, it's more than an accessory: it lights up the room.

YARN

Rowan Kid Silk Haze

A	Pearl 590	1 x 25gm
B	Majestic 589	2 x 25gm
C	Smoke 605	1 x 25gm
D	Heavenly 592	1 x 25gm
E	Meadow 581	1 x 25gm
F	Trance 582	1 x 25gm
G	Drab 588	1 x 25gm
H	Blushes 583	1 x 25gm
J	Dewberry 600	1 x 25gm

CROCHET HOOK

3.00mm (no 11) (US D3) crochet hook

TENSION

One motif measures 8.5 cm square using 3.00mm (US D3) hook.

FINISHED SIZE

Completed shawl measures 43 cm (17 in) wide and 170 cm (67 in) long, excluding fringe.

CROCHET ABBREVIATIONS

Ch = chain; **ss** = slip stitch; **dc** = double crochet; **tr** = treble; **dtr** = double treble; **sp(s)** = space(s); **tr2tog** = *yoh, insert hook into next tr, yoh and draw loop through, yoh and draw through 2 loops*, miss 2 tr, rep from * to * once more, yoh and draw through all 3 loops on hook; **yoh** = yarn over hook.

BASIC MOTIF

Using 3.00mm (US D3) hook and first colour, make 10 ch and join with a ss to form a ring.

Round 1 (RS): 3 ch (counts as first tr), 31 tr into ring, ss to top of 3 ch at beg of round.

Round 2: (7 ch, miss 3 tr, ss to next tr) 7 times, 3 ch, miss 3 tr, 1 dtr into next tr. Break off first colour and join in 2nd colour.

Round 3: 3 ch (counts as 1 tr), 6 tr into top of dtr at end of previous round, miss 3 ch, *7 tr into next ch, miss (3 ch, 1 ss and 3 ch), rep from * to end, ss to top of 3 ch at beg of round.

Round 4: Ss into next tr, 6 ch (counts as 1 tr and 3 ch), *miss 1 tr, (1 dtr, 5 ch and 1 dtr) into next tr, 3 ch, miss 1 tr, tr2tog over next 4 tr, 3 ch, miss 1 tr, 1 dc into next tr, 3 ch, miss 1 tr**, tr2tog over next 4 tr, 3 ch, rep from * to end, ending last rep at **, 1 tr into next tr, ss to 3rd of 6 ch at beg of round. Break off 2nd colour and join in 3rd colour.

Round 5: 1 ch (does NOT count as st), 1 dc into same place as ss at end of previous round, *3 dc into next ch sp, 1 dc into next dtr, 6 dc into next ch sp, 1 dc into next dtr, 3 dc into next ch sp, 1 dc into next tr2tog, 3 dc into next ch sp, 1 dc into next dc, 3 dc into next ch sp**, 1 dc into next tr2tog, rep from * to end, ending last rep at **, ss to first dc.
Fasten off.
Basic motif is a square, with 23 dc along each side.

SHAWL

Using colours of yarn at random, make 100 basic motifs.

Join motifs to form a rectangle 5 motifs wide and 20 motifs long as folls: holding motifs WS together and using yarn B, work a row of dc along edge of motifs, inserting hook through corresponding dc of both edges.

When all motifs are joined, work one round of dc using yarn B all round entire outer edge, ending with ss to first dc.
Fasten off.

Cut 35 cm lengths of yarn B and knot groups of 5 of these lengths through each ch sp along ends of shawl to form fringe.

MAGNOLIA

KIM HARGREAVES

A big roll neck, fastened by large buttons at one side, is the defining feature of this
soft, comforting jumper. The subtle juxtaposition of knitwear and a floaty, floral
skirt takes one back to an era where femininity had an effortless grace and less of
the contrivance of today.

YARN

	XS	S	M	L	XL	
To fit bust	81	86	91	97	102	cm
	32	34	36	38	40	in

Rowan Kid Classic and Kid Silk Haze

A	Classic Glacier 822						
		6	6	6	7	7	x 50gm
B	Haze Heavenly 592						
		4	4	4	5	5	x 25gm

NEEDLES

1 pair 5mm (no 6) (US 8) needles

1 pair 5½ mm (no 5) (US 9) needles

1 pair 6mm (no 4) (US 10) needles

BUTTONS – 2 x 00359

TENSION

16 sts and 20 rows to 10 cm measured over stocking stitch pattern using 6mm (US 10) needles and yarn A and yarn B HELD TOGETHER.

BACK

Cast on 76 (80: 84: 88: 92) sts using 5½ mm (US 9) needles and yarn A and yarn B HELD TOGETHER.

Row 1 (RS): K1, *P2, K2, rep from * to last 3 sts, P2, K1.

Row 2: P1, *K2, P2, rep from * to last 3 sts, K2, P1.

These 2 rows form rib.

Work in rib for a further 8 rows, ending with a WS row.

Change to 6mm (US 10) needles.

Beg with a K row, cont in st st as folls:

Work 2 rows.

Next row (dec) (RS): K2, K2tog, K to last 4 sts, K2tog tbl, K2.

Working all decreases as set by last row, dec 1 st at each end of every foll 6th row until 68 (72: 76: 80: 84) sts rem.

Work 13 rows, ending with a WS row.

Next row (inc) (RS): K2, M1, K to last 2 sts, M1, K2.

Working all increases as set by last row, inc 1 st at each end of every foll 8th row until there are 76 (80: 84: 88: 92) sts.

Cont straight until back measures 37 (38: 38: 39: 39) cm, ending with a WS row.

Shape armholes

Cast off 4 sts at beg of next 2 rows.

68 (72: 76: 80: 84) sts.

Dec 1 st at each end of next 5 (5: 7: 7: 9) rows, then on foll 0 (1: 1: 2: 2) alt rows, then on foll 4th row.

56 (58: 58: 60: 60) sts.

Cont straight until armhole measures 22 (22: 23: 23: 24) cm, ending with a WS row.

Shape shoulders and back neck

Cast off 4 sts at beg of next 2 rows.

48 (50: 50: 52: 52) sts.

Next row (RS): Cast off 4 sts, K until there are 7 sts on right needle and turn, leaving rem sts on a holder.

Work each side of neck separately.

Cast off 4 sts at beg of next row.

Cast off rem 3 sts.

With RS facing, rejoin yarns to rem sts, cast off centre 26 (28: 28: 30: 30) sts, K to end.

Complete to match first side, reversing shapings.

FRONT

Work as given for back until 10 (10: 10: 12: 12) rows less have been worked than on back to start of shoulder shaping, ending with a WS row.

Shape neck

Next row (RS): K17 (17: 17: 18: 18) and turn, leaving rem sts on a holder.

Work each side of neck separately.

Dec 1 st at neck edge of next 4 rows, then on foll 2 (2: 2: 3: 3) alt rows.

11 sts.

Work 1 row, ending with a WS row.

Shape shoulder

Cast off 4 sts at beg of next and foll alt row.

Work 1 row.

Cast off rem 3 sts.

With RS facing, rejoin yarns to rem sts, cast off centre 22 (24: 24: 24: 24) sts, K to end.

Complete to match first side, reversing shapings.

SLEEVES (both alike)

Cast on 48 (48: 48: 50: 50) sts using 5½ mm (US 9) needles and yarn A and yarn B HELD TOGETHER.

Row 1 (RS): P1 (1: 1: 2: 2), K2, *P2, K2, rep from * to last 1 (1: 1: 2: 2) sts, P1 (1: 1: 2: 2).

Row 2: K1 (1: 1: 2: 2), P2, *K2, P2, rep from * to last 1 (1: 1: 2: 2) sts, K1 (1: 1: 2: 2).

These 2 rows form rib.

Work in rib for a further 18 rows, ending with a WS row.

Change to 6mm (US 10) needles.

Beg with a K row, cont in st st as folls:

Work 4 rows.

Next row (inc) (RS): K2, M1, K to last 2 sts, M1, K2.

Working all increases as set by last row, inc 1 st at each end of every foll 20th (20th: 16th: 20th: 16th) row to 54 (54: 54: 58: 56) sts, then on every foll 18th (18th: 14th: -: 14th) row until there are 56 (56: 58: -: 60) sts.

Cont straight until sleeve measures 46 (46: 47: 47: 47) cm, ending with a WS row.

Shape top

Cast off 4 sts at beg of next 2 rows.

48 (48: 50: 50: 52) sts.

Dec 1 st at each end of next 3 rows, then on foll alt row, then on every foll 4th row until 32 (32: 34: 34: 36) sts rem.

Work 1 row, ending with a WS row.

Dec 1 st at each end of next and every foll alt row to 28 sts, then on foll 5 rows, ending with a WS row.

Cast off rem 18 sts.

MAKING UP

PRESS as described on the information page. Join both shoulder seams using back stitch, or mattress stitch if preferred.

Collar

Cast on 90 (98: 98: 106: 106) sts using 5mm (US 8) needles and yarn A and yarn B HELD TOGETHER.

Row 1 (RS): K2, (P1, K1) 3 times, P2, *K2, P2, rep from * to last 8 sts, (K1, P1) 3 times, K2.

Row 2: (K1, P1) 4 times, K2, *P2, K2, rep from * to last 8 sts, (P1, K1) 4 times.

These 2 rows form rib.

Work in rib for a further 10 rows.

Change to 6mm (US 10) needles.

Work 4 rows, ending with a WS row.

Row 17 (RS): Rib 18, M1, rib 2, M1, rib 30 (34: 34: 38: 38), M1, rib 2, M1, rib to end. 94 (102: 102: 110: 110) sts.

Keeping rib correct, work 3 rows.

Row 21: Rib 19, M1, rib 2, M1, rib 32 (36: 36: 40: 40), M1, rib 2, M1, rib to end. 98 (106: 106: 114: 114) sts.

Keeping rib correct, work 3 rows.

Row 25: Rib 20, M1, rib 2, M1, rib 34 (38: 38: 42: 42), M1, rib 2, M1, rib to end. 102 (110: 110: 118: 118) sts.

Keeping rib correct, work 3 rows.

Row 29: Rib 21, M1, rib 2, M1, rib 36 (40: 40: 44: 44), M1, rib 2, M1, rib to end. 106 (114: 114: 122: 122) sts.

Keeping rib correct, work 3 rows.

Cast off loosely in rib.

See information page for finishing instructions, setting in sleeves using the set-in method.

Overlap ends of collar for 8 sts and sew cast-on edge of collar to neck edge, positioning shaped sections at shoulder seams. Using photograph as a guide, attach buttons through both layers of collar.

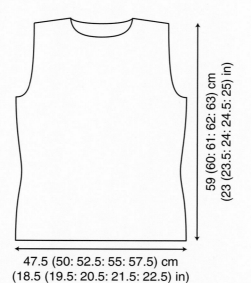

47.5 (50: 52.5: 55: 57.5) cm
(18.5 (19.5: 20.5: 21.5: 22.5) in)

59 (60: 61: 62: 63) cm
(23 (23.5: 24: 24.5: 25) in)

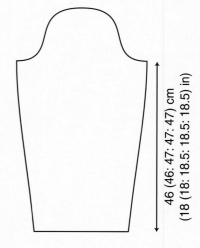

46 (46: 47: 47: 47) cm
(18 (18: 18.5: 18.5: 18.5) in)

JOY

KIM HARGREAVES

Inspired by the delightful French film Amelie, this cardigan combines refinement and naivety with its petite collar and neat buttons. The pleated skirt carries through the slim line. The ankle socks and classic beret complete the girlish look.

YARN

	XS	S	M	L	XL	
To fit bust	81	86	91	97	102	cm
	32	34	36	38	40	in

Rowan Yorkshire Tweed 4 ply

	10	10	11	11	12	x 25gm

(photographed in Enchant 268)

NEEDLES

1 pair 2³/₄ mm (no 12) (US 2) needles
1 pair 3mm (no 11) (US 2/3) needles
1 pair 3¹/₄ mm (no 10) (US 3) needles

BUTTONS – 8 x 00322

BEADS – approx 5,300 x 01020 beads

TENSION

26 sts and 38 rows to 10 cm measured over
patterned stocking stitch using 3¹/₄ mm
(US 3) needles.

SPECIAL ABBREVIATIONS

Bead 1 = place a bead by bringing yarn to front
(RS) of work and slipping bead up next to st
just worked, slip next st purlwise from left
needle to right needle and take yarn back to
back (WS) of work, leaving bead sitting in
front of slipped st on RS. Do not place beads
on edge sts of rows as this will interfere with
seaming.

Beading note: Before starting to knit, thread
beads onto yarn.
To do this, thread a fine sewing needle (one
that will easily pass through the beads) with
sewing thread.
Knot ends of thread and then pass end of
yarn through this loop. Thread a bead onto
sewing thread and then gently slide it along
and onto knitting yarn. Continue in this
way until required number of beads are
on yarn.

BACK

Cast on 113 (119: 127: 133: 141) sts using
3mm (US 2/3) needles.
Row 1 (RS): K0 (1: 1: 0: 0), *P1, K1, rep from
* to last 1 (0: 0: 1: 1) st, P1 (0: 0: 1: 1).
Rows 2 and 3: P0 (1: 1: 0: 0), *K1, P1, rep
from * to last 1 (0: 0: 1: 1) st, K1 (0: 0: 1: 1).
Row 4: As row 1.
These 4 rows form double moss st.
Work in double moss st for a further 2 rows,
ending with a WS row.
Change to 3¹/₄ mm (US 3) needles.
Cont in double moss st for a further 14 rows,
ending with a WS row.
Counting in from both ends of last row, place
markers on 28th (29th: 31st: 32nd: 34th) st in
from ends of row.
Next row (dec) (RS): Work 2 tog, *patt to within 1 st
of marked st, work 3 tog (marked st is centre st of
these 3 sts), rep from * once more, patt to last
2 sts, work 2 tog. 107 (113: 121: 127: 135) sts.
Work 9 rows.
Rep last 10 rows 3 times more, ending
with a WS row. 89 (95: 103: 109: 117) sts.
Purl 2 rows.
Starting and ending rows as indicated and
repeating the 12 patt rows throughout, cont in
patt from chart for body as folls:
Inc 1 st at each end of 3rd and every foll 4th row to
101 (107: 115: 121: 129) sts, then on every foll 6th
row until there are 113 (119: 127: 133: 141) sts.
Cont straight until back measures 35 (36: 36:
37: 37) cm, ending with a WS row.
Shape armholes
Keeping patt correct, cast off 4 (5: 5: 6: 6) sts at
beg of next 2 rows. 105 (109: 117: 121: 129) sts.
Dec 1 st at each end of next 5 (5: 7: 7: 9) rows, then
on foll 5 (6: 6: 7: 7) alt rows. 85 (87: 91: 93: 97) sts.
Cont straight until armhole measures 20 (20:
21: 21: 22) cm, ending with a WS row.
Shape shoulders and back neck
Cast off 8 (8: 9: 9: 9) sts at beg of next 2 rows.
69 (71: 73: 75: 79) sts.

Next row (RS): Cast off 8 (8: 9: 9: 9) sts, patt
until there are 12 (12: 12: 12: 14) sts on right
needle and turn, leaving rem sts on a holder.
Work each side of neck separately.
Cast off 4 sts at beg of next row.
Cast off rem 8 (8: 8: 8: 10) sts.
With RS facing, rejoin yarn to rem sts, cast off
centre 29 (31: 31: 33: 33) sts, patt to end.
Complete to match first side, reversing
shapings.

LEFT FRONT

Cast on 60 (63: 67: 70: 74) sts using 3mm
(US 2/3) needles.
Row 1 (RS): K0 (1: 1: 0: 0), *P1, K1, rep from
* to end.
Row 2: *P1, K1, rep from * to last 0 (1: 1:
0: 0) st, P0 (1: 1: 0: 0).
Row 3: P0 (1: 1: 0: 0), *K1, P1, rep from * to end.
Row 4: *K1, P1, rep from * to last 0 (1: 1: 0:
0) st, K0 (1: 1: 0: 0).
These 4 rows form double moss st.
Work in double moss st for a further 2 rows,
ending with a WS row.
Change to 3¹/₄ mm (US 3) needles.
Cont in double moss st for a further 14 rows,
ending with a WS row.
Counting in from end of last row, place marker on
28th (29th: 31st: 32nd: 34th) st in from end of row.
Next row (dec) (RS): Work 2 tog, patt to within 1
st of marked st, work 3 tog (marked st is centre st
of these 3 sts), patt to end. 57 (60: 64: 67: 71) sts.
Work 9 rows.
Rep last 10 rows 3 times more, ending with a
WS row. 48 (51: 55: 58: 62) sts.
Purl 2 rows.
Starting and ending rows as indicated and
repeating the 12 patt rows throughout, cont in
patt from chart for body as folls:
Row 1 (RS): Work first 42 (45: 49: 52: 56) sts
as row 1 of chart, double moss st 6 sts.
Row 2: Double moss st 6 sts, work last 42 (45:
49: 52: 56) sts as row 2 of chart.

These 2 rows set the sts – front opening edge 6 sts still in double moss st with rem sts in patt from chart.

Cont as set, inc 1 st at beg of next and every foll 4th row to 54 (57: 61: 64: 68) sts, then on every foll 6th row until there are 60 (63: 67: 70: 74) sts.

Cont straight until left front matches back to beg of armhole shaping, ending with a WS row.

Shape armhole

Keeping patt correct, cast off 4 (5: 5: 6: 6) sts at beg of next row. 56 (58: 62: 64: 68) sts.

Work 1 row.

Dec 1 st at armhole edge of next 5 (5: 7: 7: 9) rows, then on foll 5 (6: 6: 7: 7) alt rows. 46 (47: 49: 50: 52) sts.

Cont straight until 34 (36: 36: 38: 38) rows less have been worked than on back to start of shoulder shaping, ending with a WS row.

Shape for collar

Next row (RS): Patt to last 7 sts, double moss st 7 sts.

Next row: Double moss st 7 sts, patt to end.

Next row: Patt to last 8 sts, double moss st 8 sts.

Next row: Double moss st 8 sts, patt to end.

Next row: Patt to last 9 sts, double moss st 9 sts.

Next row: Double moss st 9 sts, patt to end.

Cont in this way, working one more st in double moss st at front opening edge on next and every foll alt row until the foll row has been worked:

Next row (WS): Double moss st 22 (23: 23: 24: 24) sts, patt to end.

Keeping sts correct as now set, work a further 2 rows, ending with a WS row.

Shape shoulder

Cast off 8 (8: 9: 9: 9) sts at beg of next and foll alt row, then 8 (8: 8: 8: 10) sts at beg of foll alt row. 22 (23: 23: 24: 24) sts.

Work 1 row, ending with a WS row.

Break yarn and leave sts on a holder.

Mark positions for 8 buttons along left front opening edge – first to come in row 45, last to come 2.5 cm below start of collar shaping, and rem 6 buttons evenly spaced between.

RIGHT FRONT

Cast on 60 (63: 67: 70: 74) sts using 3mm (US 2/3) needles.

Row 1 (RS): *K1, P1, rep from * to last 0 (1: 1: 0: 0) st, K0 (1: 1: 0: 0).

Row 2: P0 (1: 1: 0: 0), *K1, P1, rep from * to end.

Row 3: *P1, K1, rep from * to last 0 (1: 1: 0: 0) st, P0 (1: 1: 0: 0).

Row 4: K0 (1: 1: 0: 0), *P1, K1, rep from * to end.

These 4 rows form double moss st.

Work in double moss st for a further 2 rows, ending with a WS row.

Change to 3¼ mm (US 3) needles.

Cont in double moss st for a further 14 rows, ending with a WS row.

Counting in from beg of last row, place marker on 28th (29th: 31st: 32nd: 34th) st in from beg of row.

Next row (dec) (RS): Patt to within 1 st of marked st, work 3 tog (marked st is centre st of these 3 sts), patt to last 2 sts, work 2 tog. 57 (60: 64: 67: 71) sts.

Work 9 rows.

Rep last 10 rows twice more, and then first of these rows (the dec row) again. 48 (51: 55: 58: 62) sts.

Work 3 rows.

Next row (buttonhole row) (RS): Patt 2 sts, work 2 tog, yrn (to make a buttonhole), patt to end.

Work a further 5 rows, ending with a WS row.

Purl 2 rows.

Starting and ending rows as indicated and repeating the 12 patt rows throughout, cont in patt from chart for body as folls:

Row 1 (RS): Double moss st 6 sts, work last 42 (45: 49: 52: 56) sts as row 1 of chart.

Row 2: Work first 42 (45: 49: 52: 56) sts as row 2 of chart, double moss st 6 sts.

These 2 rows set the sts – front opening edge 6 sts still in double moss st with rem sts in patt from chart.

Complete to match left front, reversing shapings and with the addition of a further 7 buttonholes worked to correspond with positions marked on left front for buttons. When right front is complete, ending with a WS row, do NOT break off yarn. Set this ball of yarn to one side for collar.

SLEEVES (both alike)

Cast on 61 (61: 63: 65: 65) sts using 3¼ mm (US 3) needles.

Beg with a K row, work in st st for 2 rows, ending with a WS row.

Starting and ending rows as indicated and repeating the 12 patt rows throughout, cont in patt from chart for sleeve as folls:

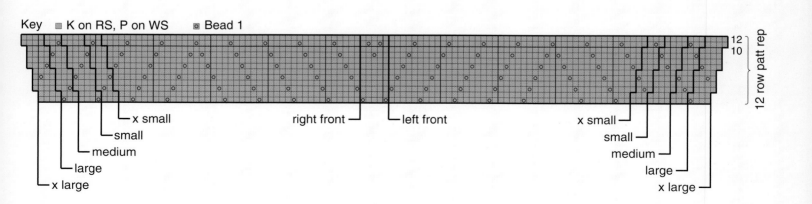

Key ◼ K on RS, P on WS   ◉ Bead 1

x small
small
medium
large
x large

right front
left front

x small
small
medium
large
x large

12
10

12 row patt rep

Inc 1 st at each end of 29th and every foll 12th (12th: 10th: 10th: 10th) row to 77 (67: 87: 89: 73) sts, then on every foll 10th (10th: 8th: 8th: 8th) row until there are 83 (85: 89: 91: 95) sts, taking inc sts into patt.

Cont straight until sleeve measures 43 (43: 44: 44: 44) cm, ending with a WS row.

Shape top

Keeping patt correct, cast off 4 (5: 5: 6: 6) sts at beg of next 2 rows.

75 (75: 79: 79: 83) sts.

Dec 1 st at each end of next 5 rows, then on foll 3 alt rows, then on every foll 4th row until 45 (45: 49: 49: 53) sts rem.

Work 1 row, ending with a WS row.

Dec 1 st at each end of next and every foll alt row to 35 sts, then on foll 3 rows, ending with a WS row.

33 sts.

Cast off rem 29 sts.

CUFFS (both alike)

Cast on 65 (65: 67: 69: 69) sts using 2³/₄mm (US 2) needles.

Row 1 (RS): P1, *K1, P1, rep from * to end.

Rows 2 and 3: K1, *P1, K1, rep from * to end.

Row 4: As row 1.

These 4 rows form double moss st.

Work in double moss st for a further 2 rows, ending with a WS row.

Starting and ending rows as indicated, cont in patt from chart for cuff as folls:

Row 1 (RS): Double moss st 5 sts, work next 55 (55: 57: 59: 59) sts as row 1 of chart, double moss st rem 5 sts.

Row 2: Double moss st 5 sts, work next 55 (55: 57: 59: 59) sts as row 2 of chart, double moss st rem 5 sts.

These 2 rows set the sts – 5 sts still in double moss st at each end and rem sts in patt foll chart.

Cont as set until all 24 rows of chart have been completed, ending with a WS row.

Cast off.

MAKING UP

PRESS as described on the information page.

Join both shoulder seams using back stitch, or mattress stitch if preferred.

Collar

With RS facing, using 3mm (US 2/3) needles and ball of yarn left with right front, patt across 22 (23: 23: 24: 24) sts on right front holder, pick up and knit 37 (39: 39: 41: 41) sts from back, then patt across 22 (23: 23: 24: 24) sts on left front holder. 81 (85: 85: 89: 89) sts.

Work in double moss st as set by front sts for 3 cm, ending with a WS row.

Cast off in double moss st.

See information page for finishing instructions, setting in sleeves using the set-in method.

Overlap ends of cuffs for 2 sts and sew together at cast-off edge. With RS of cuff against WS of sleeve and positioning ends of cuffs 7 cm back from sleeve seam, sew cast-off edge of cuffs to cast-on edge of sleeves.

Fold cuff to RS.

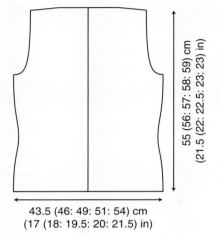

55 (56: 57: 58: 59) cm (21.5 (22: 22.5: 23: 23) in)

43.5 (46: 49: 51: 54) cm (17 (18: 19.5: 20: 21.5) in)

43 (43: 44: 44: 44) cm (17 (17: 17.5: 17.5: 17.5) in)

Sleeve chart

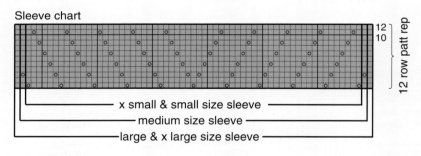

12 row patt rep

x small & small size sleeve
medium size sleeve
large & x large size sleeve

Cuff chart

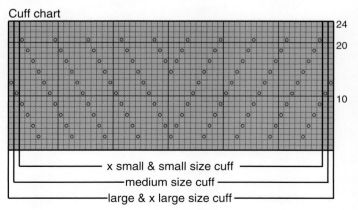

x small & small size cuff
medium size cuff
large & x large size cuff

PIERS
MARTIN STOREY

Wrap-over necks were a hallmark of the 50's and 60's. This hunky jumper, with its repeated motifs of fir trees and snowflakes, takes its inspiration from alpine winters, spent in wooden chalets fringed with icicles. It's a real open-air look that brings to mind the crunch of snow underfoot and the stars in the night sky.

YARN

	S	M	L	XL	XXL	
To fit chest	97	102	107	112	117	cm
	38	40	42	44	46	in

Rowan Yorkshire Tweed DK

A	Goose 352						
		10	11	11	12	12	x 50gm
B	Rowdy 355						
		3	3	3	3	3	x 50gm
C	Sprinkle 353						
		2	2	2	2	2	x 50gm

NEEDLES

1 pair 3¼ mm (no 10) (US 3) needles
1 pair 4mm (no 8) (US 6) needles
3¼ mm (no 10) (US 3) circular needle

TENSION

22 sts and 29 rows to 10 cm measured over
patterned stocking stitch using 4mm
(US 6) needles.

BACK

Cast on 111 (117: 123: 129: 135) sts using
3¼ mm (US 3) needles and yarn A.
Row 1 (RS): P3, *K3, P3, rep from * to end.
Row 2: K3, *P3, K3, rep from * to end.
These 2 rows form rib.
Cont in rib for a further 23 rows, ending
with a RS row.
Row 26 (WS): Rib 6 (4: 7: 6: 4), M1, *rib 11
(12: 12: 13: 14), M1, rep from * to last 6 (5: 8: 6:
5) sts, rib to end. 121 (127: 133: 139: 145) sts.
Change to 4mm (US 6) needles.
Starting and ending rows as indicated, using the
intarsia technique as described on the information
page and repeating the 76 row patt repeat
throughout, cont in patt from chart, which is
worked entirely in st st beg with a K row, as folls:
Cont straight until back measures 43 (43: 44:
44: 45) cm, ending with a WS row.
Shape armholes
Keeping patt correct, cast off 6 (6: 7: 7: 8) sts at

beg of next 2 rows. 109 (115: 119: 125: 129) sts.**
Dec 1 st at each end of next 3 (5: 5: 7: 7) rows,
then on foll 3 (3: 4: 4: 5) alt rows, then on foll
4th row. 95 (97: 99: 101: 103) sts.
Cont straight until armhole measures 22 (23:
23: 24: 24) cm, ending with a WS row.
Shape shoulders and back neck
Cast off 10 sts at beg of next 2 rows.
75 (77: 79: 81: 83) sts.
Next row (RS): Cast off 10 sts, patt until there
are 14 (14: 15: 15: 15) sts on right needle and
turn, leaving rem sts on a holder.
Work each side of neck separately.
Cast off 4 sts at beg of next row.
Cast off rem 10 (10: 11: 11: 11) sts.
With RS facing, rejoin yarns to rem sts, cast off
centre 27 (29: 29: 31: 33) sts, patt to end.
Complete to match first side, reversing shapings.

FRONT

Work as given for back to **, end with a WS row.
Dec 1 st at each end of next 3 (5: 5: 7: 7) rows,
then on foll 3 (3: 4: 4: 4) alt rows, then on foll
4th (4th: 0: 0: 0) row. 95 (97: 101: 103: 107) sts.
Work 3 (1: 3: 1: 1) rows, end with a WS row.
Divide for neck
Next row (RS): (K2tog) 0 (0: 1: 0: 1) times,
patt 31 (32: 32: 35: 35) sts and turn, leaving
rem sts on a holder. 31 (32: 33: 35: 36) sts.
Work each side of neck separately.
Dec 1 st at armhole edge on 0 (0: 0: 2nd: 4th)
row **and at same time** dec 1 st at neck edge
on 22nd (16th: 16th: 12th: 10th) and every
foll 0 (16th: 16th: 12th: 10th) row until 30 (30:
31: 31: 31) sts rem.
Cont straight until front matches back to
start of shoulder shaping, end with a WS row.
Shape shoulder
Cast off 10 sts at beg of next and foll alt row.
Work 1 row.
Cast off rem 10 (10: 11: 11: 11) sts.
With RS facing, rejoin yarns to rem sts, cast off
centre 33 sts, patt to last 0 (0: 2: 0: 2) sts,

(K2tog) 0 (0: 1: 0: 1) times.
Complete to match first side, reversing shapings.

SLEEVES (both alike)

Cast on 51 (51: 53: 55: 55) sts using 3¼ mm
(US 3) needles and yarn A.
Row 1 (RS): P0 (0: 1: 2: 2), K3, *P3, K3, rep
from * to last 0 (0: 1: 2: 2) sts, P0 (0: 1: 2: 2).
Row 2: K0 (0: 1: 2: 2), P3, *K3, P3, rep from
* to last 0 (0: 1: 2: 2) sts, K0 (0: 1: 2: 2).
These 2 rows form rib.
Cont in rib for a further 23 rows, ending
with a RS row.
Row 26 (WS): Rib 3 (3: 4: 5: 5), M1, *rib 9,
M1, rep from * to last 3 (3: 4: 5: 5) sts, rib
to end. 57 (57: 59: 61: 61) sts.
Change to 4mm (US 6) needles.
Starting and ending rows as indicated, cont
in patt from chart, shaping sides by inc 1 st
at each end of 7th (7th: 7th: 7th: 5th) and
every foll 6th (6th: 6th: 6th: 4th) row to
87 (91: 93: 93: 65) sts, then on every foll
8th (-: -: 8th: 6th) row until there are
89 (-: -: 95: 97) sts, taking inc sts into patt.
Cont straight until sleeve measures 48 (49: 49:
50: 50) cm, ending with a WS row.
Shape top
Keeping patt correct, cast off 6 (6: 7: 7: 8) sts
at beg of next 2 rows. 77 (79: 79: 81: 81) sts.
Dec 1 st at each end of next 5 rows, then on
foll 3 alt rows, then on every foll 4th row until
53 (55: 55: 57: 57) sts rem.
Work 1 row, ending with a WS row.
Dec 1 st at each end of next and every foll
alt row to 47 sts, then on foll 7 rows, ending
with a WS row. 33 sts.
Cast off 5 sts at beg of next 2 rows.
Cast off rem 23 sts.

MAKING UP

PRESS as described on the information page.
Join both shoulder seams using back stitch, or
mattress stitch if preferred.

Collar

With RS facing, using 3¹/₄ mm (US 3)
circular needle and yarn A, pick up and
knit 45 (47: 47: 49: 49) sts up right side of
neck, 39 (41: 41: 43: 43) sts from back,
then 45 (47: 47: 49: 49) sts down left side
of neck. 129 (135: 135: 141: 141) sts.
Beg with row 2, work in rib as given for back
for 15 cm.
Cast off in rib.
Overlap ends of collar and sew to front neck
cast-off sts.
See information page for finishing instructions,
setting in sleeves using the set-in method.

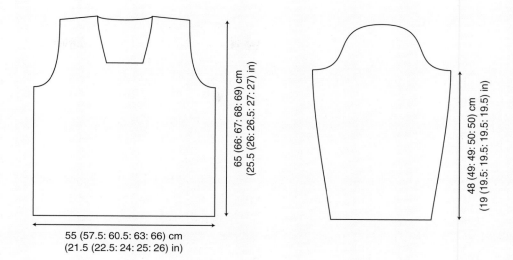

65 (66: 67: 68: 69) cm
(25.5 (26: 26.5: 27: 27) in)

55 (57.5: 60.5: 63: 66) cm
(21.5 (22.5: 24: 25: 26) in)

48 (49: 49: 50: 50) cm
(19 (19.5: 19.5: 19.5: 19.5) in)

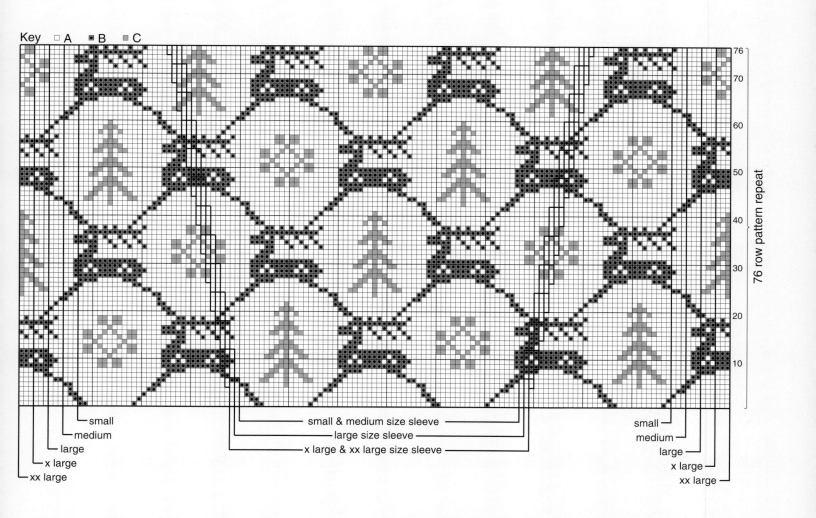

Key □ A ▪ B ▫ C

76 row pattern repeat

small
medium
large
x large
xx large

small & medium size sleeve
large size sleeve
x large & xx large size sleeve

small
medium
large
x large
xx large

MONETTE
LUCINDA GUY

This small, floaty scarf is fine and feminine.
Delightfully fluffy, it is light enough to be worn with a dress or blouse.
The lace edge enhances the delicate look of something precious.

YARN

Rowan Kid Silk Haze

A Marmalade   596 2   x 25gm
B Candy Girl   606 1   x 25gm

NEEDLES

1 pair 3¹/₄ mm (no 10) (US 3) needles

TENSION

25 sts and 34 rows to 10 cm measured over
stocking stitch using 3¹/₄ mm (US 3) needles.

FINISHED SIZE

Completed scarf measures 20 cm (8 in) wide
and 150 cm (59 in) long.

SCARF

First section

Cast on 51 sts using 3¹/₄ mm (US 3) needles
and yarn A.

Row 1 (RS): K1, *yfwd, K3, sl 1, K2tog, psso,
K3, yfwd, K1, rep from * to end.

Row 2: Purl.

Row 3: As row 1.

Row 4: Knit.

Rows 5 to 8: As rows 1 to 4.

Rows 9 to 14: Knit.

Join in yarn B.

Rows 15 and 16: Using yarn B, knit.

Rows 17 and 18: Using yarn A, knit.

Rows 19 to 22: As rows 15 to 18.

Rows 23 and 24: As rows 15 and 16.

Row 25: Using yarn A, knit.

Row 26: Using yarn A, purl.

Rows 27 to 38: As rows 15 to 26.

Rows 39 and 40: As rows 15 and 16.

Row 41: Using yarn A, knit.

Row 42: Using yarn A, purl.

Row 43: Using yarn B, knit.

Row 44: Using yarn B, purl.

Rep rows 41 to 44 **only** until first section
measures 75 cm, ending after row 43.**

Break yarn and leave sts on a holder.

Second section

Work as given for first section to **.

Join sections

Holding sections RS together and using yarn B,
cast off sts of both sections together.

MAKING UP

PRESS as described on the information page.

CHERIE

KIM HARGREAVES

The boyish look of this sweater, with its decorative buttons, creates the impression that it's been borrowed from a brother or boyfriend, or raided from clothes stashed away in the loft. It's a look that, paradoxically, enhances the femininity of the wearer - especially when, as here, it's worn next to the skin.

YARN

	XS	S	M	L	XL	
To fit bust	81	86	91	97	102	cm
	32	34	36	38	40	in

Rowan Yorkshire Tweed DK

		9	9	10	10	11	x 50gm

(photographed in Gust 354)

NEEDLES

1 pair 3³/₄ mm (no 9) (US 5) needles
1 pair 4mm (no 8) (US 6) needles

BUTTONS – 3 x 00347

TENSION

20 sts and 28 rows to 10 cm measured over stocking stitch using 4mm (US 6) needles.

BACK and FRONT (both alike)

Cast on 91 (95: 101: 105: 111) sts using 3³/₄ mm (US 5) needles.
Row 1 (RS): K1, *P1, K1, rep from * to end.
Row 2: P1, *K1, P1, rep from * to end.
These 2 rows form rib.
Work in rib for a further 24 rows, dec 1 st at each end of 19th row and ending with a WS row.
89 (93: 99: 103: 109) sts.
Change to 4mm (US 6) needles.
Beg with a K row, cont in st st as folls:
Work 4 rows.
Next row (dec) (RS): K2, K2tog, K to last 4 sts, K2tog tbl, K2.
Working all decreases as set by last row, dec 1 st at each end of foll 10th row.
85 (89: 95: 99: 105) sts.
Work 19 rows, ending with a WS row.
Next row (inc) (RS): K2, M1, K to last 2 sts, M1, K2.
Working all increases as set by last row, inc 1 st at each end of every foll 8th row until there are 95 (99: 105: 109: 115) sts.
Cont straight until work measures 35 cm, ending with a WS row.

CHERIE
KIM HARGREAVES

Shape raglan armholes

Cast off 5 sts at beg of next 2 rows.

85 (89: 95: 99: 105) sts.

XL size only

Next row (RS): K2, K2tog, K to last 4 sts, K2tog tbl, K2.

Next row: P2, P2tog tbl, P to last 4 sts, P2tog, P2.

101 sts.

All sizes

Working all raglan decreases in same way as side seam decreases, dec 1 st at each end of next and 3 (3: 1: 1: 0) foll 4th rows, then on every foll alt row until 37 (39: 39: 41: 41) sts rem.

Work 1 row, ending with a WS row.

Cast off.

SLEEVES (both alike)

Cast on 69 (69: 71: 73: 73) sts using 3³/₄ mm (US 5) needles.

Work in rib as given for back for 32 rows, dec 1 st at each end of 17th and foll 10th row and ending with a WS row.

65 (65: 67: 69: 69) sts.

Change to 4mm (US 6) needles.

Beg with a K row and working all sleeve seam decreases and increases and raglan decreases in same way as for back and front, cont in st st as folls:

Dec 1 st at each end of 5th and every foll 8th row until 59 (59: 61: 63: 63) sts rem.

Work 15 rows, ending with a WS row.

Inc 1 st at each end of next and every foll 16th (12th: 14th: 14th: 12th) row to 67 (69: 67: 69: 69) sts, then on every foll - (-: 12th: 12th: 10th) row until there are - (-: 71: 73: 75) sts.

Cont straight until sleeve measures 46 (46: 47: 47: 47) cm, ending with a WS row.

Shape raglan

Cast off 5 sts at beg of next 2 rows.

57 (59: 61: 63: 65) sts.

Dec 1 st at each end of next and every foll 4th row to 41 (43: 45: 47: 49) sts, then on every foll alt row until 17 sts rem.

Work 1 row, ending with a WS row.

Cast off.

MAKING UP

PRESS as described on the information page. Join both back and right front raglan seams using back stitch, or mattress stitch if preferred.

Neckband

With RS facing and using 3³/₄ mm (US 5) needles, pick up and knit 36 (38: 38: 40: 40) sts from front, 15 sts from right sleeve (place marker on centre st of these 15 sts), 37 (39: 39: 41: 41) sts from back, and 15 sts from left sleeve (place marker on centre st of these 15 sts), then turn and cast on 6 sts.

109 (113: 113: 117: 117) sts.

Row 1 (WS): K1, *P1, K1, rep from * to end.

Row 2: K2, *P1, K1, rep from * to last st, K1.

These 2 rows form rib.

Work in rib for 1 row more.

Row 4 (RS): *Rib to within 4 sts of marked st, work 2 tog tbl, rib 5 (marked st is centre st of these 5 sts), work 2 tog, rep from * once more, rib to end.

Work 3 rows.

Rep last 4 rows once more.

101 (105: 105: 109: 109) sts.

Row 12 (RS): *Rib to within 5 sts of marked st, work 3 tog tbl, rib 5 (marked st is centre st of these 5 sts), work 3 tog, rep from * once more, rib to end.

93 (97: 97: 101: 101) sts.

Work 5 rows.

Cast off in rib.

See information page for finishing instructions. Overlap ends of neckband for 6 sts and sew cast-on edge of neckband to inside of neck edge. Using photograph as a guide, attach buttons through both layers of neckband.

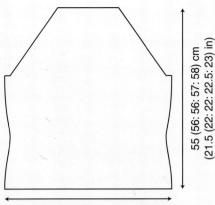

55 (56: 56: 57: 58) cm
(21.5 (22: 22: 22.5: 23) in)

47.5 (49.5: 52.5: 54.5: 57.5) cm
(18.5 (19.5: 20.5: 21.5: 22.5) in)

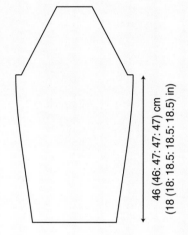

46 (46: 47: 47: 47) cm
(18 (18: 18.5: 18.5: 18.5) in)

ORIEL
KIM HARGREAVES

This neat little jacket, with its asymmetrical fastening, has a flattering neckline edged with a crocheted trim. The slightly boxy shape of the garment makes it perfect for teaming with a wide 50's style printed skirt. Here, a blouse with a lacy collar adds a finishing touch.

YARN

	XS	S	M	L	XL	
To fit bust	81	86	91	97	102	cm
	32	34	36	38	40	in

**Rowan Yorkshire Tweed 4 ply
and Kid Silk Haze**

A 4 ply Stainless 270						
	9	10	10	11	11	x 25gm
B Haze Smoke 605						
	5	5	5	6	6	x 25gm
C 4 ply Explode 277						
	1	1	1	1	1	x 25gm
D Haze Dewberry 600						
	1	1	1	1	1	x 25gm

NEEDLES

1 pair 3³/₄ mm (no 9) (US 5) needles
1 pair 4mm (no 8) (US 6) needles

CROCHET HOOK

2.50mm (no 12) (US C2) crochet hook

BUTTONS – 2 x 00348

TENSION

23 sts and 30 rows to 10 cm measured
over stocking stitch using 4mm (US 6)
needles and yarn A and B held together.

CROCHET ABBREVIATIONS

dc = double crochet; **ch** = chain;
ss = slip stitch.

BACK

Cast on 105 (111: 117: 123: 129) sts using
3³/₄ mm (US 5) needles and yarn A and B
held together.
Beg with a K row, work in st st for 6 rows,
ending with a WS row.
Change to 4mm (US 6) needles.
Cont in st st until back measures
27 (28: 28: 29: 29) cm, ending with a
WS row.

Shape armholes
Cast off 3 (4: 4: 5: 5) sts at beg of next 2 rows.
99 (103: 109: 113: 119) sts.
Dec 1 st at each end of next 5 (5: 7: 7: 9) rows,
then on foll 5 (6: 6: 7: 7) alt rows.
79 (81: 83: 85: 87) sts.
Cont straight until armhole measures 20 (20:
21: 21: 22) cm, ending with a WS row.
Shape shoulders and back neck
Cast off 7 (7: 7: 7: 8) sts at beg of next 2 rows.
65 (67: 69: 71: 71) sts.
Next row (RS): Cast off 7 (7: 7: 7: 8) sts, K
until there are 11 (11: 12: 12: 11) sts on right
needle and turn, leaving rem sts on a holder.
Work each side of neck separately.
Cast off 4 sts at beg of next row.
Cast off rem 7 (7: 8: 8: 7) sts.
With RS facing, rejoin yarns to rem sts, cast off
centre 29 (31: 31: 33: 33) sts, K to end.
Complete to match first side, reversing
shapings.

LEFT FRONT

Cast on 70 (73: 76: 79: 82) sts using 3³/₄ mm
(US 5) needles and yarn A and B held together.
Beg with a K row, work in st st for 6 rows,
ending with a WS row.
Change to 4mm (US 6) needles.
Cont in st st until left front matches back to beg
of armhole shaping, ending with a WS row.
Shape armhole
Cast off 3 (4: 4: 5: 5) sts at beg of next row.
67 (69: 72: 74: 77) sts.
Work 1 row.
Dec 1 st at armhole edge of next 5 (5: 7: 7: 9)
rows, then on foll 5 (6: 6: 7: 7) alt rows.
57 (58: 59: 60: 61) sts.
Cont straight until 29 (29: 29: 31: 31) rows less
have been worked than on back to start of
shoulder shaping, ending with a RS row.
Shape neck
Cast off 7 (8: 8: 8: 8) sts at beg of next row, 6
sts at beg of foll alt row, then 4 sts at beg of

foll 3 alt rows.
32 (32: 33: 34: 35) sts.
Dec 1 st at neck edge on next 6 rows, then on
foll 5 (5: 5: 6: 6) alt rows.
21 (21: 22: 22: 23) sts.
Work 4 rows, ending with a WS row.
Shape shoulder
Cast off 7 (7: 7: 7: 8) sts at beg of next and foll
alt row.
Work 1 row.
Cast off rem 7 (7: 8: 8: 7) sts.

RIGHT FRONT

Work to match left front, reversing shapings
and with the addition of one buttonhole worked
6 rows before start of neck shaping as folls:
Buttonhole row (RS): K3, cast off 2 sts (to
make a buttonhole – cast on 2 sts over these
cast-off sts in next row), K to end, working
armhole dec if appropriate.

SLEEVES (both alike)

Cast on 55 (55: 57: 59: 59) sts using 3³/₄ mm
(US 5) needles and yarn A and B held together.
Beg with a K row, work in st st for 6 rows,
ending with a WS row.
Change to 4mm (US 6) needles.
Cont in st st for a further 18 rows, ending
with a WS row.
Next row (RS): K2, M1, K to last 2 sts,
M1, K2.
Working all increases as set by last row, cont
in st st, shaping sides by inc 1 st at each end
of every foll 10th (10th: 10th: 10th: 8th) row
to 63 (75: 73: 75: 67) sts, then on every foll
12th (-: 12th: 12th: 10th) row until there are
73 (-: 77: 79: 81) sts.
Cont straight until sleeve measures 43 (43: 44:
44: 44) cm, ending with a WS row.
Shape top
Cast off 3 (4: 4: 5: 5) sts at beg of next 2 rows.
67 (67: 69: 69: 71) sts.
Dec 1 st at each end of next 3 rows, then on

foll 2 alt rows, then on every foll 4th row until
45 (45: 47: 47: 49) sts rem.

Work 1 row, ending with a WS row.

Dec 1 st at each end of next and every foll alt
row to 41 sts, then on foll 5 rows, ending with a
WS row.

Cast off rem 31 sts.

MAKING UP

PRESS as described on the information page.
See information page for finishing instructions,
setting in sleeves using the set-in method.

Edging

With RS facing, using 2.50mm (US C2) crochet
hook and yarn C SINGLE, attach yarn at base
of one side seam and work one round of dc
evenly around entire hem, front opening and
neck edges, working extra dc into corners,
ensuring edging lays flat and ending with ss
to first dc.

Round 2 (RS): 1 ch (does NOT count as st), 1
dc into each dc to end, working extra dc and
missing dc as required to ensure edging lays
flat, ss to first dc.

Rep last round once more, ensuring there is a
multiple of 6 sts at end of round.

Break off yarn C and join in yarn D SINGLE.

Round 4 (RS): *1 ss into each of next 3 dc,
insert hook into round 3 directly below st just
worked and draw loop through, insert hook into
round 2 one st further along and draw loop
through, insert hook into round 3 one st further
along and draw loop through, yarn over hook
and draw through all 4 loops on hook, miss 1
dc, 1 ss into each of next 2 dc, rep from * to
end, ss to first ss.

Fasten off.

Work edging around lower edge of sleeves in
same way.

Attach button to RS of left front to correspond
with buttonhole. Make button loop at top of left
front opening edge and attach button to inside
of right front to correspond.

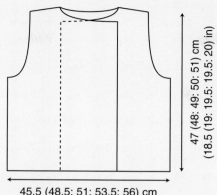

47 (48: 49: 50: 51) cm
(18.5 (19: 19.5: 19.5: 20) in)

45.5 (48.5: 51: 53.5: 56) cm
(18 (19: 20: 21: 22) in)

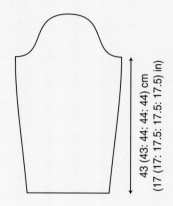

43 (43: 44: 44: 44) cm
(17 (17: 17.5: 17.5: 17.5) in)

Shape lapel

Next row (WS): P to last 6 sts, moss st 6 sts.

Next row: Moss st 7 sts, K to end.

Next row: P to last 8 sts, moss st 8 sts.

Next row: Moss st 9 sts, K to end.

Next row: P to last 10 sts, moss st 10 sts.

Cont in this way, working one extra st in moss
st on every row until there are 18 (19: 19:
20: 20) sts in moss st.

Now keeping sts correct as set, cont straight
until 7 rows less have been worked than on
back to start of shoulder shaping, ending with
a RS row.

Next row (WS): P to last 19 (20: 20: 21: 21)
sts, moss st to end.

Keeping sts correct as now set, work a further 7
rows, ending with a RS row.

Shape shoulder

Cast off 7 (7: 7: 7: 8) sts at beg of next and
foll alt row, then 7 (7: 8: 8: 7) sts at beg of foll
alt row.

19 (20: 20: 21: 21) sts.

Do NOT break yarn but leave sts on a holder –
this ball of yarn will be used for collar.

SLEEVES (both alike)

Cast on 57 (57: 59: 61: 61) sts using 3³/4 mm
(US 5) needles.

Beg with a K row, work in st st for 12 (10: 10:
10: 10) rows, ending with a WS row.

Next row (RS): K2, M1, K to last 2 sts, M1, K2.
Working all increases as set by last row, inc 1 st
at each end of every foll 12th (10th: 10th: 10th:
10th) row to 69 (65: 65: 67: 79) sts, then on
every foll 14th (12th: 12th: 12th: 12th) row
until there are 73 (75: 77: 79: 81) sts.

Cont straight until sleeve measures 36 (36: 37:
37: 37) cm, ending with a WS row.

Shape top

Cast off 4 (5: 5: 6: 6) sts at beg of next 2 rows.
65 (65: 67: 67: 69) sts.

Dec 1 st at each end of next 3 rows, then on foll
2 alt rows, then on every foll 4th row until 43
(43: 45: 45: 47) sts rem.

Work 1 row, ending with a WS row.

Dec 1 st at each end of next and every foll alt
row to 37 sts, then on foll 5 rows, end with
a WS row.

Cast off rem 27 sts.

MAKING UP

PRESS as described on the information page.
Join both shoulder seams using back stitch, or
mattress stitch if preferred.

Collar

With RS facing, using 3¹/4 mm (US 3) needles
and ball of yarn left with right front, moss st 19
(20: 20: 21: 21) sts of right front, pick up and
knit 33 (35: 35: 37: 37) sts from back, then
moss st 19 (20: 20: 21: 21) sts of left front.
71 (75: 75: 79: 79) sts.

Cont in moss st as set for 3 cm.

Cast off in moss st.

Cuffs (both alike)

Cast on 63 (63: 65: 67: 67) sts using 3¹/4 mm
(US 3) needles.

Work in moss st as given for back for 7.5 cm.

Cast off in moss st.

See information page for finishing instructions,
setting in sleeves using the set-in method. Sew cast-
on edge of left front opening border in place on
inside. Overlap ends of cuffs for 3 sts, then sew cast-
on edge of cuff to lower edge of sleeve, positioning
overlap directly opposite sleeve seam. Fold cuff to RS.

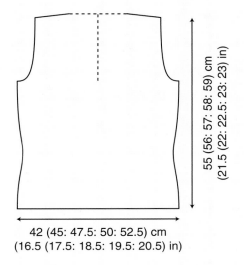

42 (45: 47.5: 50: 52.5) cm
(16.5 (17.5: 18.5: 19.5: 20.5) in)

55 (56: 57: 58: 59) cm
(21.5 (22: 22.5: 23: 23) in)

36 (36: 37: 37: 37) cm
(14 (14: 14.5: 14.5: 14.5) in)

BEAU

KIM HARGREAVES

A rustic woven effect and tweed yarn give this jumper
a rugged appearance echoing the texture of tree bark and
woodland floor. Once again, the button neckline is used to
effect for a classic of bygone times. The chunky buttons
complete the look.

YARN

	S	M	L	XL	XXL	
To fit chest	97	102	107	112	117	cm
	38	40	42	44	46	in

Rowan Yorkshire Tweed Aran

	7	7	7	8	8	x100gm

(photographed in Muffin 413)

NEEDLES

1 pair 4mm (no 8) (US 6) needles
1 pair 5mm (no 6) (US 8) needles

BUTTONS – 4 x 00341

TENSION

16 sts and 23 rows to 10 cm measured over
stocking stitch using 5mm (US 8) needles.

BACK

Cast on 90 (94: 98: 102: 106) sts using 4mm
(US 6) needles.
Row 1 (RS): K0 (2: 0: 2: 0), P2, *K2, P2, rep
from * to last 0 (2: 0: 2: 0) sts, K0 (2: 0: 2: 0).
Row 2: P0 (2: 0: 2: 0), K2, *P2, K2, rep from *
to last 0 (2: 0: 2: 0) sts, P0 (2: 0: 2: 0).
These 2 rows form rib.
Cont in rib for a further 18 rows, end with a WS row.
Change to 5mm (US 8) needles.
Starting and ending rows as indicated and
working chart rows 1 and 2 as required, cont in
patt from chart for body as folls:
Rep chart rows 1 and 2 until back measures
43 (43: 44: 44: 45) cm, ending with a WS row.
Now repeating chart rows 3 to 30 throughout,
cont as folls:
Shape armholes
Keeping patt correct, cast off 5 sts at beg of
next 2 rows. 80 (84: 88: 92: 96) sts.
Dec 1 st at each end of next 5 (5: 7: 7: 9) rows,
then on foll 2 (3: 2: 3: 2) alt rows.
66 (68: 70: 72: 74) sts.
Cont straight until armhole measures 22 (23:
23: 24: 24) cm, ending with a WS row.

BEAU

KIM HARGREAVES

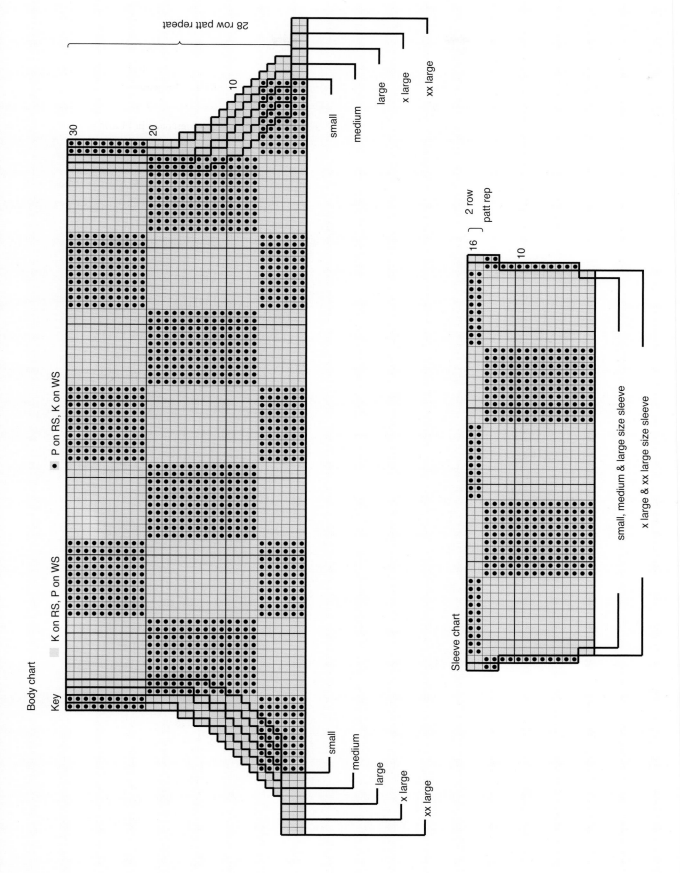

Body chart

Key

■ K on RS, P on WS

● P on RS, K on WS

28 row patt repeat

30
20
10

small
medium
large
x large
xx large

small
medium
large
x large
xx large

Sleeve chart

2 row patt rep

16
10

small, medium & large size sleeve

x large & xx large size sleeve

BEAU
KIM HARGREAVES

Shape shoulders and back neck

Cast off 6 (6: 7: 7: 7) sts at beg of next 2 rows. 54 (56: 56: 58: 60) sts.

Next row (RS): Cast off 6 (6: 7: 7: 7) sts, patt until there are 11 (11: 10: 10: 10) sts on right needle and turn, leaving rem sts on a holder.

Work each side of neck separately.

Cast off 4 sts at beg of next row.

Cast off rem 7 (7: 6: 6: 6) sts.

With RS facing, rejoin yarn to rem sts, cast off centre 20 (22: 22: 24: 26) sts, patt to end.

Complete to match first side, reversing shapings.

FRONT

Work as given for back until 34 (34: 36: 36: 36) rows less have been worked than on back to start of shoulder shaping, ending with a WS row.

Divide for front opening

Next row (RS): Patt 30 (31: 32: 33: 34) sts and turn, leaving rem sts on a holder.

Work each side of neck separately.

Work 18 rows, ending with a RS row.

Shape neck

Keeping patt correct, cast off 3 (4: 3: 4: 5) sts at beg of next row. 27 (27: 29: 29: 29) sts.

Dec 1 st at neck edge of next 6 rows, then on foll 2 (2: 3: 3: 3) alt rows. 19 (19: 20: 20: 20) sts.

Work 4 rows, ending with a WS row.

Shape shoulder

Cast off 6 (6: 7: 7: 7) sts at beg of next and foll alt row.

Work 1 row.

Cast off rem 7 (7: 6: 6: 6) sts.

With RS facing, rejoin yarn to rem sts, cast off centre 6 sts, patt to end.

Complete to match first side, reversing shapings.

SLEEVES (both alike)

Cast on 48 (48: 48: 50: 50) sts using 4mm (US 6) needles.

Row 1 (RS): K1 (1: 1: 2: 2), P2, *K2, P2, rep from * to last 1 (1: 1: 2: 2) sts, K1 (1: 1: 2: 2).

Row 2: P1 (1: 1: 2: 2), K2, *P2, K2, rep from

* to last 1 (1: 1: 2: 2) sts, P1 (1: 1: 2: 2).

These 2 rows form rib.

Cont in rib for a further 18 rows, end with a WS row.

Change to 5mm (US 8) needles.

Starting and ending rows as indicated and working chart rows 1 and 14 once only and then repeating chart rows 15 and 16 as required, cont in patt from chart for sleeve as folls:

Inc 1 st at each end of 3rd and every foll 10th row to 66 (58: 58: 58: 58) sts, then on every foll - (8th: 8th: 8th: 8th) row until there are - (68: 68: 70: 70) sts, taking inc sts into patt.

Cont straight until sleeve measures 49 (50: 50: 51: 51) cm, ending with a WS row.

Shape top

Keeping patt correct, cast off 5 sts at beg of next 2 rows. 56 (58: 58: 60: 60) sts.

Dec 1 st at each end of next 3 rows, then on foll 1 (2: 2: 3: 3) alt rows, then on every foll 4th row until 38 sts rem.

Work 1 row, ending with a WS row.

Dec 1 st at each end of next 6 rows, end with a WS row.

Cast off rem 26 sts.

MAKING UP

PRESS as described on the information page. Join both shoulder seams using back stitch, or mattress stitch if preferred.

Neckband

With RS facing and using 4mm (US 6) needles, pick up and knit 21 (22: 22: 23: 24) sts up right side of neck, 28 (30: 30: 32: 34) sts from back, then 21 (22: 22: 23: 24) sts down left side of neck. 70 (74: 74: 78: 82) sts.

Row 1 (WS): P2, *K2, P2, rep from * to end.

Row 2: K2, *P2, K2, rep from * to end.

These 2 rows form rib.

Cont in rib until neckband measures 8 cm.

Cast off in rib.

Button band

With RS facing and using 4mm (US 6) needles, pick up and knit 32 sts up right front opening edge, between cast-off sts at base of opening

and top of neckband.

Row 1 (WS): *K2, P2, rep from * to end.

This row forms rib.

Work in rib for a further 8 rows.

Cast off in rib.

Buttonhole band

With RS facing and using 4mm (US 6) needles, pick up and knit 32 sts down left front opening edge, between top of neckband and cast-off sts at base of opening.

Row 1 (WS): *P2, K2, rep from * to end.

This row forms rib.

Work in rib for a further 3 rows.

Row 5 (WS): Rib 2, *work 2 tog, yrn (to make a buttonhole), rib 6, rep from * twice more, work 2 tog, yrn (to make 4th buttonhole), rib 4.

Work in rib for a further 4 rows.

Cast off in rib.

Lay buttonhole band over button band and stitch in place to cast-off sts at base of opening.

See information page for finishing instructions, setting in sleeves using the set-in method.

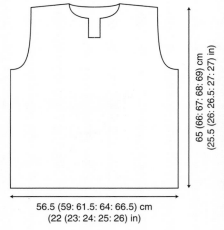

65 (66: 67: 68: 69) cm
(25.5 (26: 26.5: 27: 27) in)

56.5 (59: 61.5: 64: 66.5) cm
(22 (23: 24: 25: 26) in)

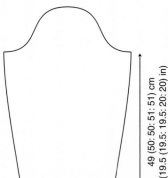

49 (50: 50: 51: 51) cm
(19.5 (19.5: 19.5: 20: 20) in)

AGNES
KIM HARGREAVES

This top, with its figure-hugging shape and banded effect, enhances a curvy hour-glass figure. The opening in the sleeves is a cheeky revealing touch that balances the demure neckline that frames the face.

AGNES
KIM HARGREAVES

YARN

	XS	S	M	L	XL	
To fit bust	81	86	91	97	102	cm
	32	34	36	38	40	in

Rowan 4 ply Soft

	6	6	7	7	7	x 50gm

(photographed in Blue Bird 369)

NEEDLES

1 pair 2³/₄ mm (no 12) (US 2) needles
1 pair 3¹/₄ mm (no 10) (US 3) needles

RIBBON – 120 (130: 130: 140: 140) cm of
1 cm wide fancy ribbon

TENSION

28 sts and 46 rows to 10 cm measured over
moss stitch, 28 sts and 36 rows to 10 cm
measured over stocking stitch using 3¹/₄ mm
(US 3) needles.

BACK

Cast on 121 (127: 135: 141: 149) sts using
2³/₄ mm (US 2) needles.
Row 1 (RS): K0 (1: 5: 0: 0), (P1, K1) 1 (2: 2:
0: 2) times, P1, *K7, (P1, K1) twice, P1, rep
from * to last 10 (1: 5: 8: 0) sts, K7 (1: 5: 7: 0),
(P1, K1) 1 (0: 0: 0: 0) times, P1 (0: 0: 1: 0).
Row 2: P0 (1: 5: 0: 0), (P1, K1) 1 (2: 2: 0: 2)
times, P1, *P7, (P1, K1) twice, P1, rep from *
to last 10 (1: 5: 8: 0) sts, P7 (1: 5: 7: 0), (P1,
K1) 1 (0: 0: 0: 0) times, P1 (0: 0: 1: 0).
These 2 rows form patt.
Work in patt for a further 6 rows, ending with a
WS row.
Change to 3¹/₄ mm (US 3) needles.
Cont in patt for a further 8 rows, ending with a
WS row.
Counting in from both ends of last row, place
markers on 22nd (25th: 29th: 32nd: 36th) and
34th (37th: 41st: 44th: 48th) sts in from both
ends of last row.
(4 marked sts.)

Next row (dec) (RS): (Patt to within 2 sts of
marked st, K2tog) twice, (patt to marked st, K
marked st, K2tog tbl) twice, patt to end.
Work 7 rows.
Rep last 8 rows 3 times more, and then first of
these rows (the dec row) again. 101 (107: 115:
121: 129) sts.
Work 19 rows, ending with a WS row.
Next row (inc) (RS): (Patt to marked st, M1, K
marked st) twice, (patt to marked st, K marked
st, M1) twice, patt to end.
Work 9 rows.
Rep last 10 rows 3 times more, and then first of
these rows (the inc row) again. 121 (127: 135:
141: 149) sts.
Cont straight until back measures 35 (36: 36:
37: 37) cm, ending with a WS row.
Shape armholes
Keeping patt correct, cast off 5 (6: 6: 7: 7) sts
at beg of next 2 rows.
111 (115: 123: 127: 135) sts.
Dec 1 st at each end of next 5 (5: 7: 7: 9) rows,
then on foll 4 (5: 5: 6: 6) alt rows. 93 (95: 99:
101: 105) sts.
Next row (WS): P1 (0: 0: 1: 1), *K1, P1, rep
from * to last 0 (1: 1: 0: 0) st, K0 (1: 1: 0: 0).
Next row: P1 (0: 0: 1: 1), *K1, P1, rep from *
to last 0 (1: 1: 0: 0) st, K0 (1: 1: 0: 0).
Last 2 rows form moss st.
Cont in moss st until armhole measures 18 (18:
19: 19: 20) cm, ending with a WS row.
Shape shoulders and back neck
Cast off 7 (7: 8: 8: 9) sts at beg of next 2 rows.
79 (81: 83: 85: 87) sts.
Next row (RS): Cast off 7 (7: 8: 8: 9) sts, moss
st until there are 12 sts on right needle and
turn, leaving rem sts on a holder.
Work each side of neck separately.
Cast off 4 sts at beg of next row.
Cast off rem 8 sts.
With RS facing, rejoin yarn to rem sts, cast off
centre 41 (43: 43: 45: 45) sts, moss st to end.
Complete to match first side.

FRONT

Work as given for back until 28 (28: 28: 30: 30)
rows less have been worked than on back to
start of shoulder shaping, end with a WS row.
Shape front neck
Next row (RS): Moss st 36 (36: 38: 39: 41) sts
and turn, leaving rem sts on a holder.
Work each side of neck separately.
Dec 1 st at neck edge of next 8 rows, then on
foll 5 (5: 5: 6: 6) alt rows, then on foll 4th row.
22 (22: 24: 24: 26) sts.
Work 5 rows, ending with a WS row.
Shape shoulder
Cast off 7 (7: 8: 8: 9) sts at beg of next and foll
alt row.
Work 1 row.
Cast off rem 8 sts.
With RS facing, rejoin yarn to rem sts, cast off
centre 21 (23: 23: 23: 23) sts, moss st to end.
Complete to match first side.

SLEEVES (both alike)

Cast on 79 (81: 85: 87: 91) sts using 2³/₄ mm
(US 2) needles.
Work in garter st for 3 rows.
Change to 3¹/₄ mm (US 3) needles.
Row 4 (eyelet row) (WS): K1, *yfwd, K2tog,
rep from * to end.
Change to 2³/₄ mm (US 2) needles.
Work in garter st for 2 rows.
Change to 3¹/₄ mm (US 3) needles.
Row 7 (RS): Knit.
Row 8: P1, *K1, P1, rep from * to end.
Row 8 sets position of moss st.
Keeping moss st correct throughout, cont as folls:
Divide for opening
Next row (RS): Moss st 39 (40: 42: 43: 45) sts
and turn, leaving rem sts on a holder.
Work each side of sleeve separately.
Work 1 row, ending with a WS row.
Inc 1 st at beg of next and every foll 6th row
until there are 43 (44: 46: 47: 49) sts.
Work 7 rows, ending with a WS row.

Shape top

Cast off 5 (6: 6: 7: 7) sts at beg of next row.

38 (38: 40: 40: 42 sts.

Work 1 row.

Dec 1 st at beg of next row and at same edge
on foll 2 rows, then on foll 2 alt rows, then on
foll 4th row. 32 (32: 34: 34: 36) sts.

Work 1 row, ending with a WS row.

Break yarn and leave sts on a second holder.

With RS facing, rejoin yarn to sts left on first
holder, work 2 tog, moss st to end.

39 (40: 42: 43: 45) sts.

Work 1 row, ending with a WS row.

Inc 1 st at end of next and every foll 6th row
until there are 43 (44: 46: 47: 49) sts.

Work 8 rows, ending with a WS row.

Shape top

Cast off 5 (6: 6: 7: 7) sts at beg of next row.

38 (38: 40: 40: 42 sts.

Dec 1 st at end of next row and at same edge
on foll 2 rows, then on foll 2 alt rows, then on
foll 4th row. 32 (32: 34: 34: 36) sts.

Work 1 row, ending with a WS row.

Break yarn.

Join sections

Next row (RS): Moss st across first 31 (31: 33:
33: 35) sts of first section, inc in last st, then
moss st across 32 (32: 34: 34: 36) sts of second
section.

65 (65: 69: 69: 73) sts.

Work 1 row, ending with a WS row.

Dec 1 st at each end of next and foll 4th row,
then on every foll 6th row to 57 (57: 61: 61:
65) sts, then on foll 4th row.

55 (55: 59: 59: 63) sts.

Work 3 rows, ending with a WS row.

Dec 1 st at each end of next and every foll alt
row to 47 sts, then on foll 5 rows, ending with
a WS row. 37 sts.

Cast off 4 sts at beg of next 2 rows.

Cast off rem 29 sts.

MAKING UP

PRESS as described on the information page.

Join right shoulder seam using back stitch, or
mattress stitch if preferred.

Neckband

With RS facing and using 2³/₄ mm (US 2)
needles, pick up and knit 25 (25: 25: 27: 27) sts
down left side of front neck, 21 (23: 23: 23: 23)
sts from front, 25 (25: 25: 27: 27) sts up right
side of front neck, then 49 (51: 51: 53: 53) sts
from back.

120 (124: 124: 130: 130) sts.

Work in garter st for 2 rows, ending with
a RS row.

Change to 3¹/₄ mm (US 3) needles.

Row 3 (eyelet row) (WS): K1, *yfwd, K2tog,
rep from * to last st, K1.

Change to 2³/₄ mm (US 2) needles.

Work in garter st for 3 rows.

Cast off knitwise (on WS).

See information page for finishing instructions,
setting in sleeves using the set-in method.

Thread ribbon through eyelet rows of sleeves
and neckband, joining ends on inside and
ensuring ribbon around neckband is long
enough to go over head.

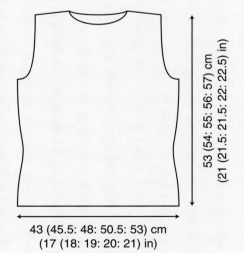

53 (54: 55: 56: 57) cm
(21 (21.5: 21.5: 22: 22.5) in)

43 (45.5: 48: 50.5: 53) cm
(17 (18: 19: 20: 21) in)

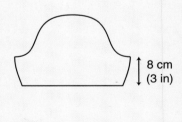

8 cm
(3 in)

DEMI
KIM HARGREAVES

The rugged Aran-inspired style of this jumper is made
delightful by the shoulder fastening and the lacy collar
peeping out beneath the neckline. The cloche hat makes
the whole look both playful and original.

YARN

	XS	S	M	L	XL	
To fit bust	81	86	91	97	102	cm
	32	34	36	38	40	in

Rowan Yorkshire Tweed Aran

	6	6	7	7	7	x100gm

(photographed in Darkside 414)

NEEDLES

1 pair 4mm (no 8) (US 6) needles
1 pair 4¹/₂ mm (no 7) (US 11) needles
1 pair 5mm (no 6) (US 8) needles
Cable needle

BUTTONS - 4 x 00339

TENSION

16 sts and 23 rows to 10 cm measured over stocking stitch using 5mm (US 8) needles.

SPECIAL ABBREVIATIONS

Cr2R = slip next st onto cable needle and leave at back of work, K1 tbl, then P1 from cable needle.

Cr2L = slip next st onto cable needle and leave at front of work, P1, then K1 tbl from cable needle.

Cr3R = slip next st onto cable needle and leave at back of work, (K1 tbl) twice, then P1 from cable needle.

Cr3L = slip next 2 sts onto cable needle and leave at front of work, P1, then (K1 tbl) twice from cable needle.

C3B = slip next st onto cable needle and leave at back of work, (K1 tbl) twice, then K1 tbl from cable needle.

C3F = slip next 2 sts onto cable needle and leave at front of work, K1 tbl, then (K1 tbl) twice from cable needle.

MB = (K1, P1, K1, P1, K1) all into next st, turn, P5, turn, lift 2nd, 3rd, 4th then 5th st over first st and then K rem st tbl.

BACK

Cast on 91 (95: 99: 103: 107) sts using 4¹/₂ mm (US 7) needles.

Starting and ending rows as indicated, work in patt foll chart for body as folls:

Work 18 rows, ending with a WS row.

Change to 5mm (US 8) needles.

Work 2 rows, ending after chart row 20.

Now repeating chart rows 21 to 44 **only** over centre sts and chart rows 21 to 40 **only** over side sts, cont foll chart as folls:

Work 2 rows.

Dec 1 st at each end of next and every foll 4th row until 83 (87: 91: 95: 99) sts rem.

Work 15 rows, ending with a WS row.

Inc 1 st at each end of next and every foll 8th row until there are 91 (95: 99: 103: 107) sts, taking inc sts into patt.

Cont straight until back measures 36 (37: 37: 38: 38) cm, ending with a WS row.

Shape armholes

Keeping patt correct, cast off 5 sts at beg of next 2 rows.

81 (85: 89: 93: 97) sts.

Dec 1 st at each end of next 5 (5: 7: 7: 9) rows, then on foll 3 (4: 4: 5: 5) alt rows.

65 (67: 67: 69: 69) sts.

Cont straight until armhole measures 20 (20: 21: 21: 22) cm, ending with a WS row.

Shape shoulders and back neck

Cast off 5 sts at beg of next 2 rows.

55 (57: 57: 59: 59) sts.

Next row (RS): Cast off 5 sts, patt until there are 10 sts on right needle and turn, leaving rem sts on a holder.

Work each side of neck separately.

Cast off 4 sts at beg of next row.

Cast off rem 6 sts.

With RS facing, rejoin yarn to rem sts, cast off centre 25 (27: 27: 29: 29) sts, patt to end.

Complete to match first side, reversing shapings.

FRONT

Work as given for back until 14 rows less have been worked than on back to start of shoulder shaping, ending with a WS row.

Shape neck

Next row (RS): Patt 23 sts and turn, leaving rem sts on a holder.

Work each side of neck separately.

Dec 1 st at neck edge of next 3 rows, ending with a WS row. 20 sts.

Make a note of exactly which patt row has just been completed and whereabouts in patt these sts sit – you will need this for shoulder section.

Cast off.

With RS facing, rejoin yarn to rem sts, cast off centre 19 (21: 21: 23: 23) sts, patt to end.

23 sts.

Dec 1 st at neck edge on next 5 rows, then on foll 2 alt rows. 16 sts.

Work 5 rows, ending with a RS row.

Shape shoulder

Cast off 5 sts at beg of next and foll alt row.

Work 1 row.

Cast off rem 6 sts.

Left front shoulder section

Cast on 20 sts using 5mm (US 8) needles.

Starting at exactly the point in patt and across row as where left shoulder was cast-off, cont in patt as folls:

Dec 1 st at neck edge (end of first row) of next 2 rows, then on foll 2 alt rows.

16 sts.

Work 4 rows, ending with a WS row.

Shape shoulder

Cast off 5 sts at beg of next and foll alt row.

Work 1 row.

Cast off rem 6 sts.

SLEEVES (Both alike)

Cast on 61 (61: 63: 63: 65) sts using 4¹/₂ mm (US 7) needles.

Row 1 (RS): P1 (1: 0: 0: 1), (K1 tbl, P1) 6 (6:

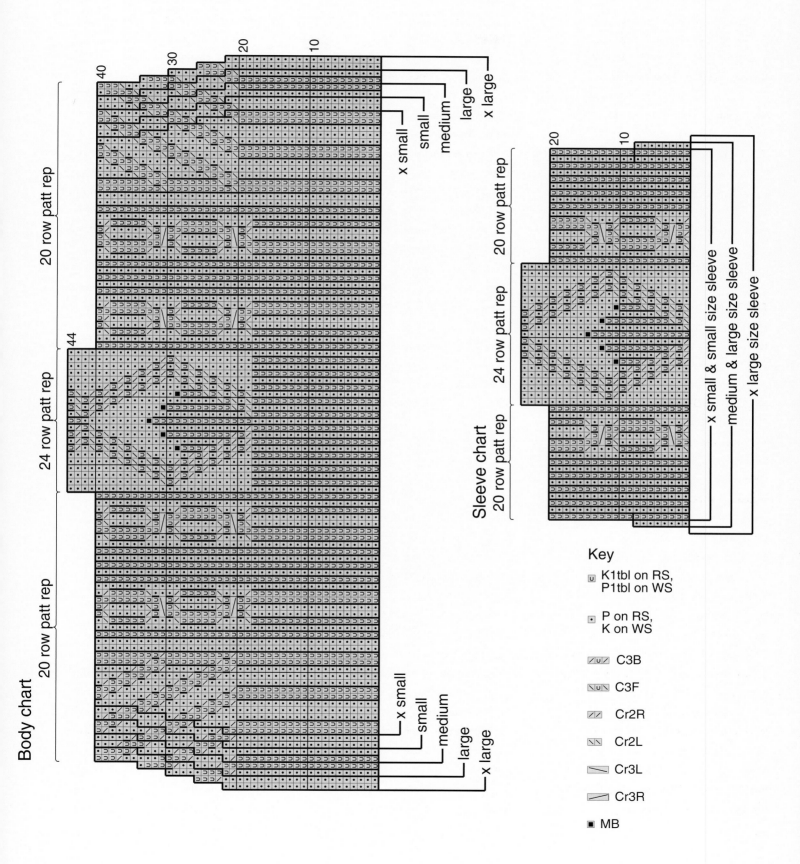

Body chart

20 row patt rep
20 row patt rep
24 row patt rep
20 row patt rep

44
40
30
20
10

x small
small
medium
large
x large

x small
small
medium
large
x large

Sleeve chart

20 row patt rep
24 row patt rep
20 row patt rep

20
10

x small & small size sleeve
medium & large size sleeve
x large size sleeve

Key

u	K1tbl on RS, P1tbl on WS
·	P on RS, K on WS
⟋u⟋	C3B
⟍u⟍	C3F
⟋⟋	Cr2R
⟍⟍	Cr2L
⟋	Cr3L
⟋	Cr3R
■	MB

7: 7: 7) times, (K1 tbl) twice, P2, (K1 tbl, P1)
13 times, K1 tbl, P2, (K1 tbl) twice, (P1, K1
tbl) 6 (6: 7: 7: 7) times, P1 (1: 0: 0: 1).

Row 2: K1 (1: 0: 0: 1), (P1 tbl, K1) 6 (6: 7: 7:
7) times, (P1 tbl) twice, K2, (P1 tbl, K1) 13
times, P1 tbl, K2, (P1 tbl) twice, (K1, P1 tbl) 6
(6: 7: 7: 7) times, K1 (1: 0: 0: 1).

These 2 rows form rib.

Cont in rib, dec 1 st at each end of 9th and every
foll 8th row until 55 (55: 57: 57: 59) sts rem.

Work 7 rows, ending with a WS row.

(34 rows of rib completed.)

Change to 5mm (US 8) needles.

Starting and ending rows as indicated, repeating
chart rows 1 to 24 **only** over centre sts and
chart rows 1 to 20 **only** over side sts, work in
patt foll chart for sleeve as folls:

Dec 1 st at each end of next and foll 8th row.

51 (51: 53: 53: 55) sts.

Work 13 rows, ending with a WS row.

Inc 1 st at each end of next and every foll 6th
row to 57 (57: 57: 57: 59) sts, then on every foll
8th row until there are 63 (63: 65: 65: 67) sts,
taking inc sts into rib.

Cont straight until sleeve measures 45 (45: 46:
46: 46) cm, ending with a WS row.

Shape top

Keeping patt correct, cast off 5 sts at beg of
next 2 rows.

53 (53: 55: 55: 57) sts.

Dec 1 st at each end of next 3 rows, then on foll
alt row, then on every foll 4th row until
37 (37: 39: 39: 41) sts rem.

Work 1 row, ending with a WS row.

Dec 1 st at each end of next and every foll alt
row to 33 sts, then on foll 5 rows, ending with a
WS row.

Cast off rem 23 sts.

MAKING UP

PRESS as described on the information page.

Join both shoulder seams using back stitch, or
mattress stitch if preferred.

Left front shoulder buttonhole band

Cast on 9 sts using 4mm (US 6) needles.

Row 1 (RS): K1, (K1 tbl, P1) 3 times,
K1 tbl, K1.

Row 2: K1, (P1 tbl, K1) 4 times.

These 2 rows form rib.

Work in rib for a further 8 rows, ending
with a WS row.

Row 11 (buttonhole row) (RS): Rib 3, work 2
tog, yrn (to make a buttonhole), rib 4.

Work 7 rows.

Rep last 8 rows once more, ending with
a WS row.

Do NOT break yarn.

Neckband

With RS facing and using 4mm (US 6)
needles, work across 9 sts of buttonhole
band as folls: rib 3, work 2 tog, yrn (to
make 3rd buttonhole), rib 4, pick up and
knit 4 sts down left side of neck, 13 (15:
15: 17: 17) sts from front, 16 sts up right
side of neck, 26 (28: 28: 30: 30) sts from
back, then 13 sts down left side of neck
to cast-on edge of left front shoulder section.
81 (85: 85: 89: 89) sts.

Row 1 (WS): K1, *P1 tbl, K1, rep from
* to end.

Row 2: K1, *K1 tbl, P1, rep from * to last 2
sts, K1 tbl, K1.

These 2 rows form rib.

Cont in rib for a further 5 rows.

Row 8 (RS): rib 3, work 2 tog, yrn (to make
4th buttonhole), rib to end.

Work in rib for a further 3 rows.

Cast off in rib.

Slip st edge of left front shoulder buttonhole
band to cast-off edge of left front shoulder.

Lay buttonhole band over left front shoulder
section so that buttonhole band seam
matches cast-on edge and sew together at
armhole edge.

See information page for finishing instructions,
setting in sleeves using the set-in method.

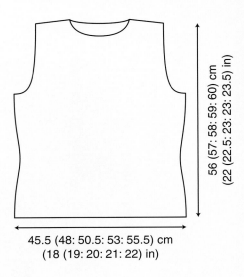

45.5 (48: 50.5: 53: 55.5) cm
(18 (19: 20: 21: 22) in)

56 (57: 58: 59: 60) cm
(22 (22.5: 23: 23: 23.5) in)

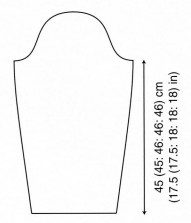

45 (45: 46: 46: 46) cm
(17.5 (17.5: 18: 18: 18) in)

TOUSCON SCAPE
BRANDON MABLY

This jacket is a celebration of rich, dark colours, drawn in broad strokes to make merging stripes. The colours remind us of the palettes of 20th century European artists such as Pierre Bonnard and Toulouse-Lautrec.

TOUSCON SCAPE
BRANDON MABLY

YARN

	XS	S	M	L	XL	
To fit bust	81	6	91	97	102	cm
	32	34	36	38	40	in

Rowan Yorkshire Tweed Chunky, Aran and DK

A	Chunky	Coast 555					
			3	4	4	4	4	x100gm

B *Aran Maze 415

			3	3	3	3	3	x100gm

C *DK Lime Leaf 348

			3	3	3	3	3	x 50gm

D *Aran Muffin 413

			3	3	3	3	3	x100gm

E Chunky Damp 550

			2	2	2	2	2	x100gm

F Chunky Pecan 553

			2	2	2	2	2	x100gm

G *DK Cheer 343

			2	2	2	2	2	x 50gm

H Chunky String 551

			2	2	2	2	2	x100gm

*Use Yorkshire Tweed Aran and
DK DOUBLE throughout

NEEDLES

1 pair 7mm (no 2) (US 10$^{1}/_{2}$) needles
1 pair 8mm (no 0) (US 11) needles

BUTTONS - 5 x 00340

TENSION

12 sts and 16 rows to 10 cm measured over
patterned stocking stitch using 8mm (US 11)
needles.

BACK

Cast on 69 (71: 75: 77: 81) sts using 7mm
(US 10$^{1}/_{2}$) needles and yarn A.
Beg with a K row, work in st st for 9 rows,
ending with a RS row.
Row 10: Knit (to form fold line).
Change to 8mm (US 11) needles.
Starting and ending rows as indicated and using

the **intarsia** technique as described on the
information page, cont in patt from chart, which is
worked entirely in st st beg with a K row, as folls:
Dec 1 st at each end of 15th and every foll 12th
row until 63 (65: 69: 71: 75) sts rem.
Work 17 rows, ending with a WS row.
Inc 1 st at each end of next and every foll 8th
row until there are 69 (71: 75: 77: 81) sts,
taking inc sts into patt.
Cont straight until chart row 82 (84: 84: 86: 86)
has been completed, ending with a WS row.
(Back should measure 51 (53: 53: 54: 54) cm
from fold line.)
Shape armholes
Keeping patt correct, cast off 5 sts at beg of
next 2 rows. 59 (61: 65: 67: 71) sts.
Dec 1 st at each end of next 3 (3: 5: 5: 7) rows,
then on foll 2 alt rows, then on foll 4th row.
47 (49: 49: 51: 51) sts.
Cont straight until chart row 120 (122: 124: 126:
128) has been completed, ending with a WS row.
(Armhole should measure 24 (24: 25: 25: 26) cm.)
Shape shoulders and back neck
Next row (RS): Cast off 7 sts, patt until there
are 10 sts on right needle and turn, leaving rem
sts on a holder.
Work each side of neck separately.
Cast off 3 sts at beg of next row.
Cast off rem 7 sts.
With RS facing, rejoin yarns to rem sts, cast off
centre 13 (15: 15: 17: 17) sts, patt to end.
Complete to match first side, reversing shapings.

LEFT FRONT

Cast on 36 (37: 39: 40: 42) sts using 7mm
(US 10$^{1}/_{2}$) needles and yarn A.
Beg with a K row, work in st st for 9 rows,
ending with a RS row.
Row 10: Knit (to form fold line).
Change to 8mm (US 11) needles.
Starting and ending rows as indicated, cont in
patt from chart as folls:
Dec 1 st at beg of 15th and every foll 12th row

until 33 (34: 36: 37: 39) sts rem.
Work 17 rows, ending with a WS row.
Inc 1 st at beg of next and every foll 8th row
until there are 36 (37: 39: 40: 42) sts, taking
inc sts into patt.
Cont straight until left front matches back to
beg of armhole shaping, ending with a WS row.
Shape armhole
Keeping patt correct, cast off 5 sts at beg of
next row. 31 (32: 34: 35: 37) sts.
Work 1 row.
Dec 1 st at armhole edge of next 3 (3: 5: 5: 7)
rows, then on foll 2 alt rows, then on foll 4th row.
25 (26: 26: 27: 27) sts.
Cont straight until chart row 109 (111: 113: 115:
117) has been completed, ending with a RS row.
Shape neck
Keeping patt correct, cast off 6 (7: 7: 8: 8) sts
at beg of next row. 19 sts.
Dec 1 st at neck edge on next 3 rows, then on
foll 2 alt rows. 14 sts.
Work 3 rows, ending with chart row 120 (122:
124: 126: 128) and a WS row.
Shape shoulder
Cast off 7 sts at beg of next row.
Work 1 row.
Cast off rem 7 sts.

RIGHT FRONT

Cast on 36 (37: 39: 40: 42) sts using 7mm
(US 10$^{1}/_{2}$) needles and yarn A.
Beg with a K row, work in st st for 9 rows,
ending with a RS row.
Row 10: Knit (to form fold line).
Change to 8mm (US 11) needles.
Starting and ending rows as indicated, cont in
patt from chart as folls:
Dec 1 st at end of 15th and foll 0 (12th: 12th:
12th: 12th) row.
35 (35: 37: 38: 40) sts.
Work 11 (1: 3: 5: 7) rows, ending with a WS row.
Next row (buttonhole row) (RS): Patt 2 sts, cast
off 2 sts (to make a buttonhole – cast on 2 sts

over these cast-off sts on next row), patt to last 2 (0: 0: 0: 0) sts, (work 2 tog) 1 (0: 0: 0: 0) times. 34 (35: 37: 38: 40) sts.

Dec 1 st at end of 12th (10th: 8th: 6th: 4th) row. 33 (34: 36: 37: 39) sts.

Making a further 4 buttonholes on every foll 20th row from previous buttonhole, complete to match left front, reversing shapings.

SLEEVES (both alike)

Cast on 33 (33: 33: 35: 35) sts using 7mm (US 10½) needles and yarn A.

Beg with a K row, work in st st for 9 rows, ending with a RS row.

Row 10: Knit (to form fold line).

Change to 8mm (US 11) needles.

Starting and ending rows as indicated, cont in patt from chart as folls:

Inc 1 st at each end of 11th and every foll 10th (10th: 8th: 10th: 8th) row to 39 (39: 37: 39: 39) sts, then on every foll 12th (12th: 10th: 12th:

10th) row until there are 45 (45: 47: 47: 49) sts, taking inc sts into patt.

Cont straight until chart row 74 (74: 76: 76: 76) has been completed, ending with a WS row. (Sleeve should measure 46 (46: 48: 48: 48) cm from fold line.)

Shape top

Keeping patt correct, cast off 5 sts at beg of next 2 rows. 35 (35: 37: 37: 39) sts.

Dec 1 st at each end of next 3 rows, then on foll alt row, then on every foll 4th row until 21 (21: 23: 23: 25) sts rem.

Work 1 row, ending with a WS row.

Dec 1 st at each end of next and every foll alt row to 15 sts, then on foll row, end with a WS row.

Cast off rem 13 sts.

MAKING UP

PRESS as described on the information page.

Join both shoulder seams using back stitch, or mattress stitch if preferred.

Front bands (both alike)

With RS facing, using 7mm (US 10 1/2) needles and yarn A, pick up and knit 81 (83: 84: 86: 87) sts along front opening edge, between fold line row and neck shaping.

Work in garter st for 2 rows.

Cast off knitwise (on WS).

Collar

With RS facing, using 7mm (US 10 1/2) needles and yarn A, starting and ending at front opening edges, pick up and knit 19 (20: 20: 21: 21) sts up right side of neck, 21 (23: 23: 25: 25) sts from back, then 19 (20: 20: 21: 21) sts down left side of neck.

59 (63: 63: 67: 67) sts.

Work in garter st for 28 rows.

Cast off knitwise.

See information page for finishing instructions, setting in sleeves using the set-in method. Fold first 9 rows of sleeves and body to inside along fold line rows and stitch in place.

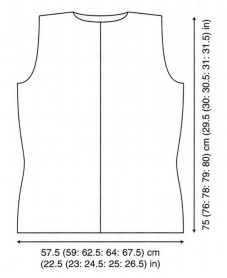

57.5 (59: 62.5: 64: 67.5) cm
(22.5 (23: 24.5: 25: 26.5) in)

75 (76: 78: 79: 80) cm (29.5 (30: 30.5: 31: 31.5) in)

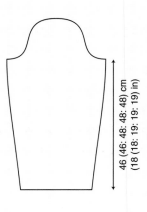

46 (46: 48: 48: 48) cm
(18 (18: 19: 19: 19) in)

TOUSCON SCAPE
BRANDON MABLY

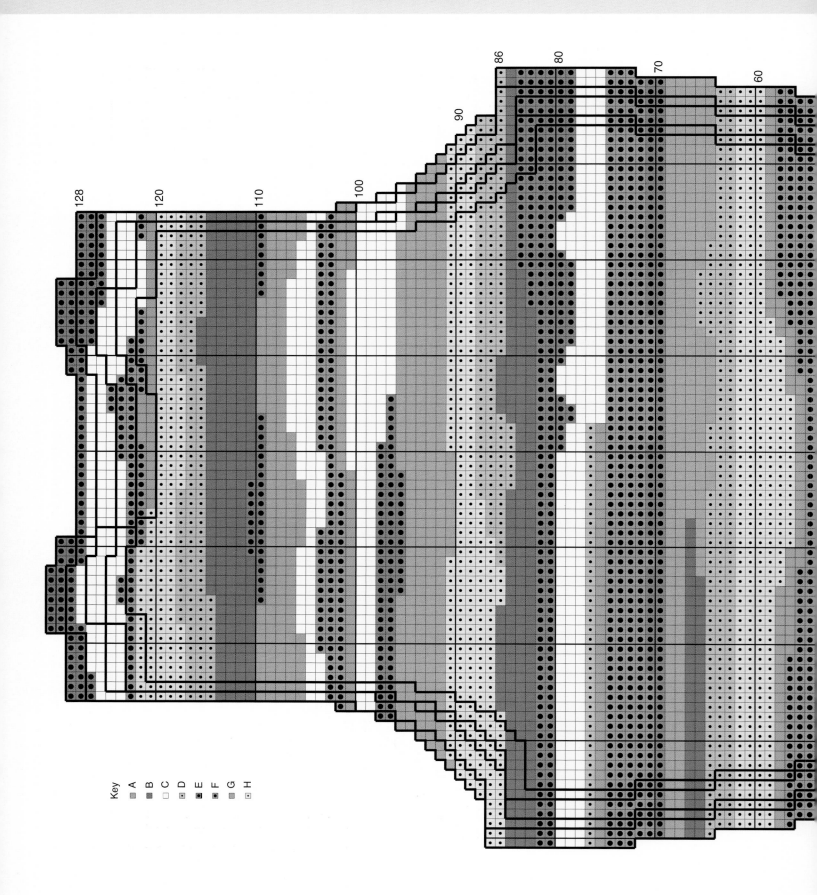

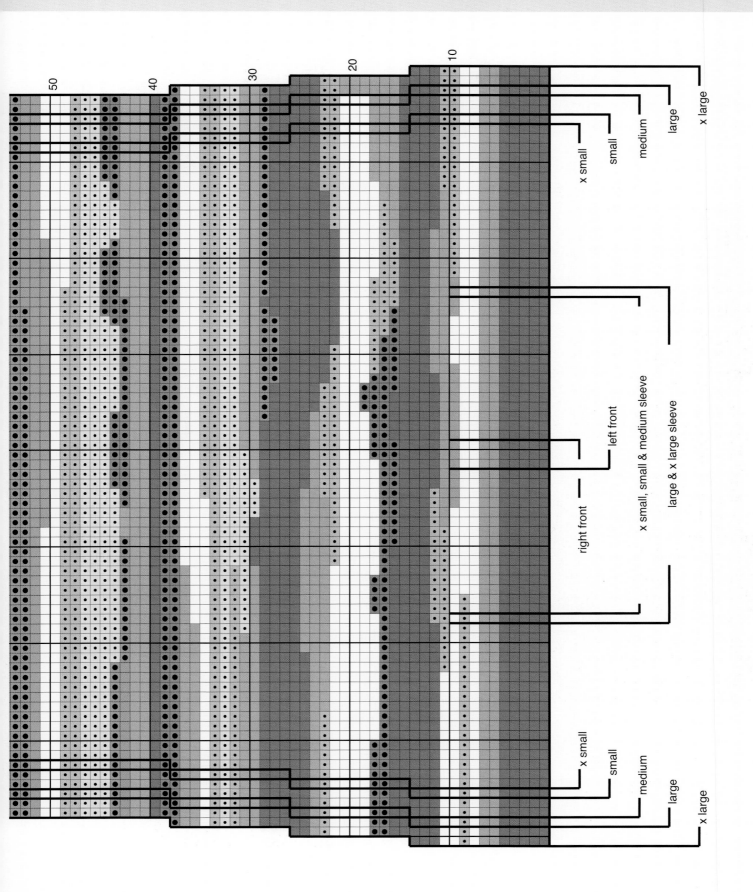

50

40

30

20

10

x small

small

medium

large

x large

right front

left front

x small, small & medium sleeve

large & x large sleeve

x small

small

medium

large

x large

109

CHARLOT
MARTIN STOREY

At once sweet and sophisticated, this cardigan has a delicacy, created by the embroidered decoration on the textured background, with the yarn giving a subtle sheen. Here, the red polka-dot dress perfectly brings out the red used for the flowers.

YARN

	XS	S	M	L	XL	
To fit bust	81	86	91	97	102	cm
	32	34	36	38	40	in

Rowan 4 ply Soft

		XS	S	M	L	XL	
A	Buzz 375	10	10	11	11	12	x 50gm
B	Goblin 379	1	1	1	1	1	x 50gm
C	Honk 374	1	1	1	1	1	x 50gm
D	Splash 373	1	1	1	1	1	x 50gm
E	Wink 377	1	1	1	1	1	x 50gm

NEEDLES

1 pair 2³/₄ mm (no 12) (US 2) needles
1 pair 3¹/₄ mm (no 10) (US 3) needles
Cable needle

BUTTONS – 8 x 00322

TENSION

28 sts and 36 rows to 10 cm measured over stocking stitch using 3¹/₄ mm (US 3) needles.

SPECIAL ABBREVIATIONS

Cr2R = slip next st onto cable needle and leave at back of work, K1 tbl, then P1 from cable needle.
Cr2L = slip next st onto cable needle and leave at front of work, P1, then K1 tbl from cable needle.
MB = (K1, P1, K1) all into next st, turn, P3, turn, K3, turn, P3, turn, sl 1, K2tog, psso.

BACK

Cast on 107 (113: 121: 127: 135) sts using 2³/₄ mm (US 2) needles and yarn A.
Row 1 (RS): K1 (0: 2: 0: 0), P3 (1: 3: 2: 0), *K3, P3, rep from * to last 1 (4: 2: 5: 3) sts, K1 (3: 2: 3: 3), P0 (1: 0: 2: 0).

Row 2: P1 (0: 2: 0: 0), K3 (1: 3: 2: 0), *P3, K3, rep from * to last 1 (4: 2: 5: 3) sts, P1 (3: 2: 3: 3), K0 (1: 0: 2: 0).

These 2 rows form rib.

Cont in rib for 9 cm, ending with a RS row.

Next row (WS): Inc in first st, rib 26 (29: 33: 36: 40), M1, (rib 1, M1) twice, rib 21, M1, (rib 1, M1) twice, rib 3, M1, (rib 1, M1) twice, rib 21, M1, (rib 1, M1) twice, rib to last st, inc in last st.

121 (127: 135: 141: 149) sts.

Change to 3¼ mm (US 3) needles.

Starting and ending rows as indicated, working chart rows 1 and 2 once only and then repeating chart rows 3 to 38 throughout, cont in patt from chart for body as folls:

Inc 1 st at each end of 9th and every foll 8th row until there are 135 (141: 149: 155: 163) sts, taking inc sts into rev st st.

Cont straight until back measures 28 (29: 29: 30: 30) cm, ending with a WS row.

Shape armholes

Keeping patt correct, cast off 5 (6: 6: 7: 7) sts at beg of next 2 rows.

125 (129: 137: 141: 149) sts.

Dec 1 st at each end of next 5 (5: 7: 7: 9) rows, then on foll 3 (4: 4: 5: 5) alt rows, then on every foll 4th row until 105 (107: 111: 113: 117) sts.

Cont straight until armhole measures 20 (20: 21: 21: 22) cm, ending with a WS row.

Shape shoulders and back neck

Cast off 9 (9: 10: 10: 11) sts at beg of next 2 rows.

87 (89: 91: 93: 95) sts.

Next row (RS): Cast off 9 (9: 10: 10: 11) sts, patt until there are 14 sts on right needle and turn, leaving rem sts on a holder.

Work each side of neck separately.

Cast off 4 sts at beg of next row.

Cast off rem 10 sts.

With RS facing, rejoin yarn to rem sts, cast off centre 41 (43: 43: 45: 45) sts dec 6 sts evenly,

patt to end.

Complete to match first side, reversing shapings.

LEFT FRONT

Cast on 54 (57: 61: 64: 68) sts using 2¾ mm (US 2) needles and yarn A.

Row 1 (RS): K1 (0: 2: 0: 0), P3 (1: 3: 2: 0), *K3, P3, rep from * to last 2 sts, K2.

Row 2: P2, K3, *P3, K3, rep from * to last 1 (4: 2: 5: 3) sts, P1 (3: 2: 3: 3), K0 (1: 0: 2: 0).

These 2 rows form rib.

Cont in rib for 9 cm, ending with a RS row.

Next row (WS): Rib 2, M1, (rib 1, M1) twice, rib 21, M1, (rib 1, M1) twice, rib to last st, inc in last st.

61 (64: 68: 71: 75) sts.

Change to 3¼ mm (US 3) needles.

Starting and ending rows as indicated, cont in patt from chart for body as folls:

Inc 1 st at beg of 9th and every foll 8th row until there are 68 (71: 75: 78: 82) sts.

Cont straight until left front matches back to beg of armhole shaping, ending with a WS row.

Shape armhole

Keeping patt correct, cast off 5 (6: 6: 7: 7) sts at beg of next row.

63 (65: 69: 71: 75) sts.

Work 1 row.

Dec 1 st at armhole edge of next 5 (5: 7: 7: 9) rows, then on foll 3 (4: 4: 5: 5) alt rows, then on every foll 4th row until 53 (54: 56: 57: 59) sts.

Cont straight until 21 (21: 21: 23: 23) rows less have been worked than on back to start of shoulder shaping, ending with a RS row.

Shape neck

Keeping patt correct, cast off 8 (9: 9: 9: 9)sts at beg of next row, then 5 sts at beg of foll alt row.

40 (40: 42: 43: 45) sts.

Dec 1 st at neck edge on next 7 rows, then on foll 5 (5: 5: 6: 6) alt rows.

28 (28: 30: 30: 32) sts.

Work 1 row, ending with a WS row.

Shape shoulder

Cast off 9 (9: 10: 10: 11) sts at beg of next and foll alt row.

Work 1 row.

Cast off rem 10 sts.

RIGHT FRONT

Cast on 54 (57: 61: 64: 68) sts using 2¾ mm (US 2) needles and yarn A.

Row 1 (RS): K2, P3, *K3, P3, rep from * to last 1 (4: 2: 5: 3) sts, K1 (3: 2: 3: 3), P0 (1: 0: 2: 0).

Row 2: P1 (0: 2: 0: 0), K3 (1: 3: 2: 0), *P3, K3, rep from * to last 2 sts, P2.

These 2 rows form rib.

Cont in rib for 9 cm, ending with a RS row.

Next row (WS): Inc in first st, rib 26 (29: 33: 36: 40), M1, (rib 1, M1) twice, rib 21, M1, (rib 1, M1) twice, rib 2.

61 (64: 68: 71: 75) sts.

Change to 3¼ mm (US 3) needles.

Starting and ending rows as indicated, cont in patt from chart for body as folls:

Inc 1 st at end of 9th and every foll 8th row until there are 68 (71: 75: 78: 82) sts.

Complete to match left front, reversing shapings.

SLEEVES (both alike)

Cast on 63 (63: 65: 67: 67) sts using 2 3/4mm (US 2) needles and yarn A.

Row 1 (RS): P0 (0: 1: 2: 2), *K3, P3, rep from * to last 3 (3: 4: 5: 5) sts, K3, P0 (0: 1: 2: 2).

Row 2: K0 (0: 1: 2: 2), *P3, K3, rep from * to last 3 (3: 4: 5: 5) sts, P3, K0 (0: 1: 2: 2).

These 2 rows form rib.

Cont in rib for 9 cm, ending with a RS row.

Next row (WS): Inc in first st, rib 27 (27: 28: 29: 29), M1, (rib 1, M1) twice, rib 3, M1, (rib 1, M1) twice, rib to last st, inc in last st.

71 (71: 73: 75: 75) sts.

Change to 3¼ mm (US 3) needles.

Starting and ending rows as indicated, working

chart rows 1 and 2 once only and then repeating chart rows 3 to 38 throughout, cont in patt from chart for sleeve as folls:

Inc 1 st at each end of 7th (5th: 5th: 5th: 5th) and every foll 8th (6th: 6th: 6th: 6th) row to 93 (75: 81: 83: 99) sts, then on every foll 10th (8th: 8th: 8th: 8th) row until there are 97 (99: 103: 105: 109) sts, taking inc sts into rev st st.

Cont straight until sleeve measures 44 (44: 45: 45: 45) cm, ending with a WS row.

Shape top

Keeping patt correct, cast off 5 (6: 6: 7: 7) sts at beg of next 2 rows.

87 (87: 91: 91: 95) sts.

Dec 1 st at each end of next 5 rows, then on foll 4 alt rows, then on every foll 4th row until 59 (59: 63: 63: 67) sts rem.

Work 1 row, ending with a WS row.

Dec 1 st at each end of next and every foll alt row to 47 sts, then on foll 7 rows, end with a WS row.

Cast off rem 33 sts, dec 6 sts evenly.

MAKING UP

PRESS as described on the information page. Join both shoulder seams using back stitch, or mattress stitch if preferred.

Neckband

With RS facing, using 2³/₄ mm (US 2) needles and yarn A, starting and ending at front opening edges, pick up and knit 33 (34: 34: 37: 37) sts up right side of neck, 47 (51: 51: 51: 51) sts from back, then 33 (34: 34: 37: 37) sts down left side of neck. 113 (119: 119: 125: 125) sts.

Body chart

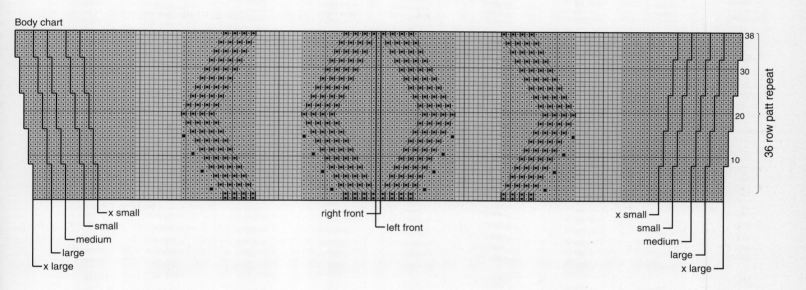

Key

☐ K on RS,
   P on WS

⊡ P on RS,
   K on WS

⊙ K1 tbl on RS,
   P1 tbl on WS

■ MB

▨ Cr2R

▧ Cr2L

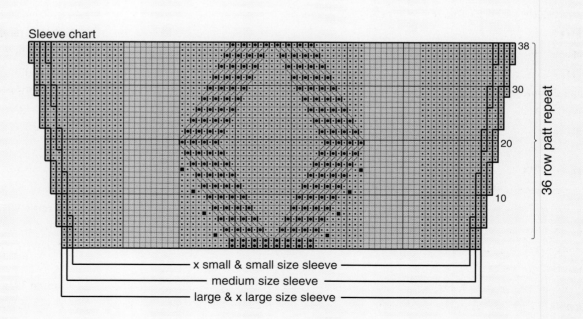

Row 1 (WS): K1, *P3, K3, rep from * to last 4 sts, P3, K1.

Row 2: K4, *P3, K3, rep from * to last st, K1.

These 2 rows form rib.

Work in rib for a further 3 rows.

Cast off in rib.

Button band

With RS facing, using 2³/4 mm (US 2) needles and yarn A, pick up and knit 131 (131: 137: 137: 137) sts down left front opening edge, between top of neckband and cast-on edge.

Work in rib as given for neckband for 5 rows.

Cast off in rib.

Buttonhole band

With RS facing, using 2³/4 mm (US 2) needles and yarn A, pick up and knit 131 (131: 137: 137: 137) sts up right front opening edge, between cast-on edge and top of neckband.

Work in rib as given for neckband for 3 rows.

Row 4 (RS): Rib 2 (2: 3: 3: 3), work 2 tog, yrn (to make a buttonhole), (rib 10, work 2 tog, yrn) twice, *rib 18 (18: 19: 19: 19), work 2 tog, yrn, rep from * to last 3 sts, rib 3.

Work in rib for 1 row more.

Cast off in rib.

Embroidery

Following diagram, embroider design onto fronts.

See information page for finishing instructions, setting in sleeves using the set-in method.

Embroidery Diagram

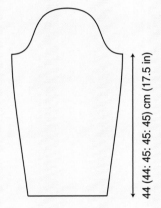

48 (49: 50: 51: 52) cm
(19 (19.5: 19.5: 20: 20.5) in)

44 (46: 49: 51: 54) cm
(17.5 (18: 19.5: 20: 21.5) in)

44 (44: 45: 45: 45) cm (17.5 in)

RIVA

KIM HARGREAVES

The long lines of this jacket, worn with a soft blouse, make it an elegant,
flattering shape that skims the body. Here it's set off by a large corsage that
picks up the colour of the skirt.

YARN

	XS	S	M	L	XL	
To fit bust	81	86	91	97	102	cm
	32	34	36	38	40	in

Rowan Yorkshire Tweed Chunky

	11	11	12	13	13	x100gm

(photographed in Stout 554)

Oddments of Yorkshire Tweed 4 ply in four shades and oddment of Kidsilk Haze for Corsage

NEEDLES

1 pair 7mm (no 2) (US 10 1/2) needles
1 pair 8mm (no 0) (US 11) needles
1 pair 3¼ mm (no 10) (US 3) needles

TENSION

12 sts and 16 rows to 10 cm measured over moss stitch using 8mm (US 11) needles.

BACK

Cast on 71 (73: 77: 79: 83) sts using 8mm (US 11) needles.
Row 1 (RS): K1, *P1, K1, rep from * to end.
Row 2: As row 1.
These 2 rows form moss st.
Cont in moss st until back measures 63 (64: 64: 65: 65) cm, ending with a WS row.
Shape armholes
Keeping moss st correct, cast off 3 sts at beg of next 2 rows.
65 (67: 71: 73: 77) sts.
Dec 1 st at each end of next 5 (5: 7: 7: 9) rows, then on foll alt row, then on foll 4th row.
51 (53: 53: 55: 55) sts.
Cont straight until armhole measures 22 (22: 23: 23: 24) cm, ending with a WS row.
Shape shoulders and back neck
Cast off 6 sts at beg of next 2 rows.
39 (41: 41: 43: 43) sts.
Next row (RS): Cast off 6 sts, moss st until there are 9 sts on right needle and turn, leaving rem sts on a holder.

Work each side of neck separately.
Cast off 4 sts at beg of next row.
Cast off rem 5 sts.
With RS facing, rejoin yarn to rem sts, cast off centre 9 (11: 11: 13: 13) sts, moss st to end.
Complete to match first side, reversing shapings.

LEFT FRONT

Cast on 36 (37: 39: 40: 42) sts using 8mm (US 11) needles.
Row 1 (RS): *K1, P1, rep from * to last 0 (1: 1: 0: 0) st, K0 (1: 1: 0: 0).
Row 2: K0 (1: 1: 0: 0), *P1, K1, rep from * to end.
These 2 rows form moss st.
Cont in moss st until left front matches back to beg of armhole shaping, ending with a WS row.
Shape armhole
Keeping moss st correct, cast off 3 sts at beg of next row.
33 (34: 36: 37: 39) sts.
Work 1 row.
Dec 1 st at armhole edge of next 5 (5: 7: 7: 9) rows, then on foll alt row, then on foll 4th row.
26 (27: 27: 28: 28) sts.
Cont straight until 13 rows less have been worked than on back to start of shoulder shaping, ending with a RS row.
Shape neck
Next row (WS): Moss st 3 (4: 4: 5: 5) sts and slip these sts onto a holder, moss st to end.
23 sts.
Dec 1 st at neck edge on next 4 rows, then on foll alt row, then on foll 4th row. 17 sts.
Work 2 rows, ending with a WS row.
Shape shoulder
Cast off 6 sts at beg of next and foll alt row.
Work 1 row.
Cast off rem 5 sts.

RIGHT FRONT

Cast on 36 (37: 39: 40: 42) sts using 8mm

(US 11) needles.
Row 1 (RS): K0 (1: 1: 0: 0), *P1, K1, rep from * to end.
Row 2: *K1, P1, rep from * to last 0 (1: 1: 0: 0) st, K0 (1: 1: 0: 0).
These 2 rows form moss st.
Complete to match left front, reversing shapings.

SLEEVES (both alike)

Cast on 35 (35: 35: 37: 37) sts using 8mm (US 11) needles.
Work in moss st as given for back, shaping sides by inc 1 st at each end of 17th (17th: 15th: 17th: 17th) and every foll 16th (16th: 14th: 16th: 14th) row to 41 (41: 39: 45: 41) sts, then on every foll 14th (14th: 12th: -: 12th) row until there are 43 (43: 45: -: 47) sts, taking inc sts into moss st.
Cont straight until sleeve measures 44 (44: 45: 45: 45) cm, ending with a WS row.
Shape top
Keeping moss st correct, cast off 3 sts at beg of next 2 rows.
37 (37: 39: 39: 41) sts.
Dec 1 st at each end of next 3 rows, then on foll alt row, then on every foll 4th row until 23 (23: 25: 25: 27) sts rem.
Work 1 row, ending with a WS row.
Dec 1 st at each end of next and every foll alt row to 17 sts, then on foll row, ending with a WS row.
Cast off rem 15 sts.

MAKING UP

PRESS as described on the information page.
Join both shoulder seams using back stitch, or mattress stitch if preferred.
Neckband
With RS facing and using 7mm (US 10 ½) needles, slip 3 (4: 4: 5: 5) sts left on right front holder onto right needle, rejoin yarn and pick up and knit 16 sts up right side of neck, 17 (19:

19: 21: 21) sts from back, and 16 sts down left side of neck, then moss st 3 (4: 4: 5: 5) sts from left front holder.

55 (59: 59: 63: 63) sts.

Cast off knitwise (on WS).

See information page for finishing instructions, setting in sleeves using the set-in method.

CORSAGE
BACK SECTION

Using 3¼ mm (US 3) needles and first shade of Yorkshire Tweed 4 ply, cast on 28 sts.

Beg with a K row and working in 2 row stripes of first and second shades, cont in st st until work is a perfect square.

Cast off.

FRONT SECTION

Work as for back section but using third and fourth shades of Yorkshire Tweed 4 ply.

CENTRE SECTION

Cast on 6 sts using Kidsilk Haze DOUBLE and 3¼ mm (US 3) needles.

Cont in rev st st, inc 1 st at end of next 6 rows.

12 sts.

Dec 1 st at end of next 6 rows.

6 sts.

Cast off.

MAKING UP

Machine hot wash and tumble dry back and front sections to shrink and felt them.

Once dry, press. From back section, cut a 7.5 cm diameter circle, and from front section, cut a 6 cm diameter circle. Run gathering threads around outer edge of centre section and pull up so that centre section forms a soft, flat ball.

Fasten ends off securely.

Lay front section onto back section, and run gathering threads through both layers around centre point. Pull up threads so that sections form a rumpled flower shape and fasten ends off securely. Position centre section over these gathering threads and sew all 3 sections together at centre. If desired, attach a safety pin or brooch back to back of corsage.

85 (86: 87: 88: 89) cm (33.5 (34: 34: 34.5: 35) in)

59 (61: 64: 66: 69) cm
(23 (24: 25: 26: 27) in)

43 (43: 44: 44: 44) cm
(17 (17: 17.5: 17.5: 17.5) in)

JARRETT
KIM HARGREAVES

This jacket, knitted up in a tweedy natural yarn and with shoulder patches, has a real artisan feel. It's a look favoured by intellectuals, painters and writers striving to rediscover nature and return to the simple life.

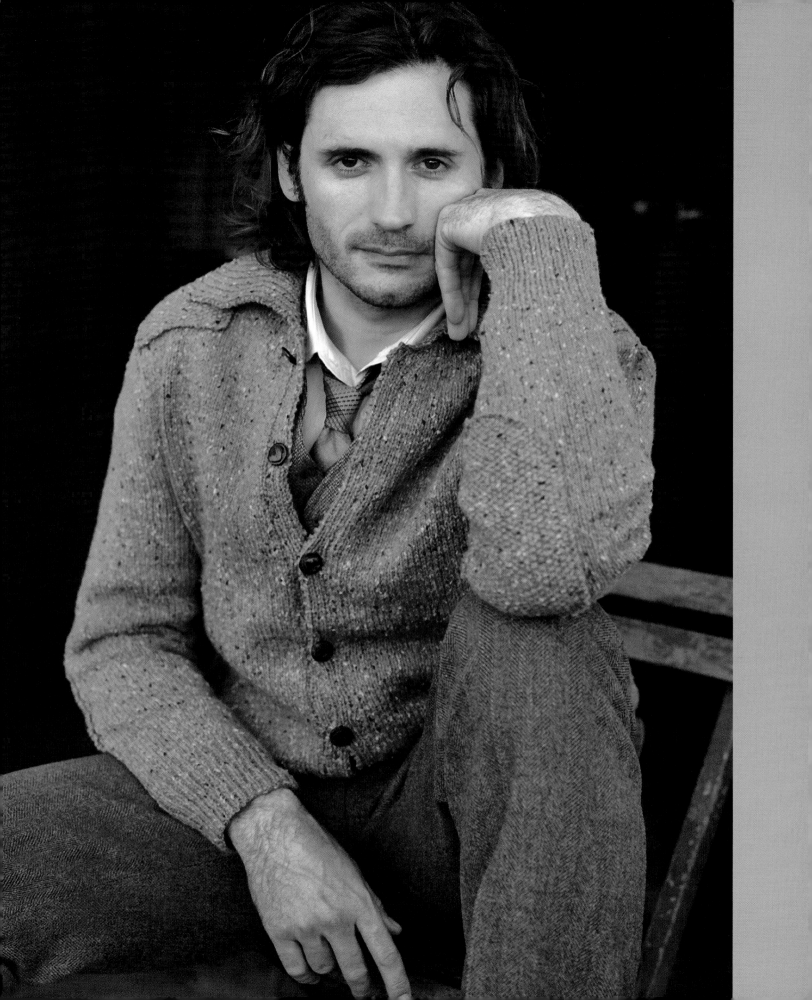

YARN

	S	M	L	XL	XXL	
To fit chest	97	102	107	112	117	cm
	38	40	42	44	46	in

Rowan Yorkshire Tweed DK

	13	14	15	16	16	x 50gm

(photographed in Sprinkle 353)

NEEDLES

1 pair 3¼ mm (no 10) (US 3) needles
1 pair 3¾ mm (no 9) (US 5) needles
1 pair 4mm (no 8) (US 6) needles

BUTTONS – 7 x 00340 buttons

TENSION

20 sts and 28 rows to 10 cm measured over stocking stitch using 4mm (US 6) needles.

BACK

Cast on 113 (117: 123: 127: 133) sts using 3¾ mm (US 5) needles.
Row 1 (RS): K1, *P1, K1, rep from * to end.
Row 2: P1, *K1, P1, rep from * to end.
These 2 rows form rib.
Cont in rib for a further 24 rows, ending with a WS row.
Change to 4mm (US 6) needles.
Beg with a K row, cont in st st until back measures 43 (43: 44: 44: 45) cm, ending with a WS row.
Shape armholes
Cast off 5 (5: 6: 6: 7) sts at beg of next 2 rows. 103 (107: 111: 115: 119) sts.
Dec 1 st at each end of next 5 (7: 7: 9: 9) rows, then on foll 2 (1: 2: 1: 2) alt rows, then on every foll 4th row until 85 (87: 89: 91: 93) sts rem.
Cont straight until armhole measures 22 (23: 23: 24: 24) cm, ending with a WS row.
Shape shoulders and back neck
Cast off 8 sts at beg of next 2 rows. 69 (71: 73: 75: 77) sts.

Next row (RS): Cast off 8 sts, K until there are 12 (12: 13: 13: 13) sts on right needle and turn, leaving rem sts on a holder.
Work each side of neck separately.
Cast off 4 sts at beg of next row.
Cast off rem 8 (8: 9: 9: 9) sts.
With RS facing, rejoin yarn to rem sts, cast off centre 29 (31: 31: 33: 35) sts, K to end.
Complete to match first side, reversing shapings.

LEFT FRONT

Cast on 64 (66: 68: 70: 74) sts using 3¾ mm (US 5) needles.
Row 1 (RS): *K1, P1, rep from * to last 2 sts, K2.
Row 2: *K1, P1, rep from * to end.
These 2 rows form rib.
Cont in rib for a further 4 rows, ending with a WS row.
Row 7 (RS): Rib to last 4 sts, yrn, P2tog, K2.
Cont in rib for a further 18 rows, ending with a RS row.
Row 26 (WS): Rib 7 and slip these 7 sts onto a holder, rib to last 0 (0: 1: 1: 0) st, (inc in last st) 0 (0: 1: 1: 0) times. 57 (59: 62: 64: 67) sts.
Change to 4mm (US 6) needles.
Beg with a K row, cont in st st until left front matches back to beg of armhole shaping, ending with a WS row.
Shape armhole
Cast off 5 (5: 6: 6: 7) sts at beg of next row. 52 (54: 56: 58: 60) sts.
Work 1 row.
Dec 1 st at armhole edge of next 5 (7: 7: 9: 9) rows, then on foll 2 (1: 2: 1: 2) alt rows, then on every foll 4th row until 43 (44: 45: 46: 47) sts rem.
Cont straight until 21 (21: 23: 23: 23) rows less have been worked than on back to start of shoulder shaping, ending with a RS row.
Shape neck
Cast off 7 (8: 7: 8: 9) sts at beg of next row. 36 (36: 38: 38: 38) sts.

Dec 1 st at neck edge of next 8 rows, then on foll 3 (3: 4: 4: 4) alt rows, then on foll 4th row. 24 (24: 25: 25: 25) sts.
Work 2 rows, ending with a WS row.
Shape shoulder
Cast off 8 sts at beg of next and foll alt row.
Work 1 row.
Cast off rem 8 (8: 9: 9: 9) sts.

RIGHT FRONT

Cast on 64 (66: 68: 70: 74) sts using 3¾ mm (US 5) needles.
Row 1 (RS): K2, *P1, K1, rep from * to end.
Row 2: *P1, K1, rep from * to end.
These 2 rows form rib.
Cont in rib for a further 23 rows, ending with a RS row.
Row 26 (WS): (Inc in first st) 0 (0: 1: 1: 0) times, rib to last 7 sts and turn, leaving last 7 sts on a holder.
57 (59: 62: 64: 67) sts.
Complete to match left front, reversing shapings.

SLEEVES (both alike)

Cast on 59 (59: 61: 63: 63) sts using 3¾ mm (US 5) needles.
Work in rib as given for back for 26 rows, ending with a WS row.
Change to 4mm (US 6) needles.
Beg with a K row, work in st st for 2 rows, ending with a WS row.
Row 29 (RS): K2, M1, K to last 2 sts, M1, K2.
Working all increases as set by last row, cont in st st, shaping sides by inc 1 st at each end of every foll 8th row to 65 (73: 75: 75: 85) sts, then on every foll 10th row until there are 81 (83: 85: 87: 89) sts.
Cont straight until sleeve measures 49 (50: 50: 51: 51) cm, ending with a WS row.
Shape top
Cast off 5 (5: 6: 6: 7) sts at beg of next 2 rows. 71 (73: 73: 75: 75) sts.

Dec 1 st at each end of next 3 rows, then on foll 2 alt rows, then on every foll 4th row until 47 (49: 49: 51: 51) sts rem.

Work 1 row, ending with a WS row.

Dec 1 st at each end of next and foll 0 (1: 1: 2: 2) alt rows, then on foll 5 rows, ending with a WS row.

Cast off rem 35 sts.

MAKING UP

PRESS as described on the information page.

Shoulder patches (make 4)

Cast on 25 (25: 27: 27: 27) sts using 3¹/₄ mm (US 3) needles.

Row 1: K1, *P1, K1, rep from * to end.

Row 2: As row 1.

These 2 rows form moss st.

Work in moss st for a further 38 rows.

Cast off 8 (8: 9: 9: 9) sts at beg of next and foll alt row.

Work 1 row.

Cast off rem 9 sts.

Lay shoulder patches onto RS of back and front, matching shaped cast-off edges and positioning patch 2 sts in from armhole edge. Sew in place.

Join both shoulder seams using back stitch, or mattress stitch if preferred, enclosing shoulder patches in seam.

Button band

Slip 7 sts left on right front holder onto 3³/₄ mm (US 5) needles and rejoin yarn with WS facing.

Cont in rib as set until button band, when slightly stretched, fits up right front opening edge to neck shaping, ending with a WS row.

Cast off in rib.

Mark positions for 7 buttons on this band – first to come level with buttonhole already worked in left front, last to come 1.5 cm below neck shaping and rem 5 buttons evenly spaced between.

Buttonhole band

Slip 7 sts left on left front holder onto 3³/₄ mm

(US 5) needles and rejoin yarn with RS facing.

Cont in rib as set until buttonhole band, when slightly stretched, fits up left front opening edge to neck shaping, ending with a WS row and with the addition of a further 6 buttonholes worked to correspond with positions marked for buttons on right front as folls:

Buttonhole row (RS): P1, K1, P1, yrn, P2tog, K2.

When band is complete, cast off in rib.

Slip st bands in place.

Collar

With RS facing and using 3³/₄ mm (US 5) needles, starting and ending halfway across top of bands, pick up and knit 34 (35: 36: 37: 38) sts up right side of neck, 37 (39: 39: 41: 43) sts from back, then 34 (35: 36: 37: 38) sts down left side of neck. 105 (109: 111: 115: 119) sts.

Row 1 (WS of body, RS of collar): K2, *P1, K1, rep from * to last st, K1.

Row 2: K1, *P1, K1, rep from * to end.

These 2 rows form rib.

Cont in rib until collar measures 14 cm.

Cast off in rib.

Elbow patches (make 2)

Cast on 9 sts using 3¹/₄ mm (US 3) needles.

Work in moss st as given for shoulder patches for 1 row.

Keeping moss st correct, cast on 3 sts at beg of next 2 rows. 15 sts.

Inc 1 st at beg of next 8 rows. 23 sts.

Work 2 rows.

Inc 1 st at beg of next 2 rows. 25 sts.

Work 24 rows.

Dec 1 st at beg of next 2 rows. 23 sts.

Work 2 rows.

Dec 1 st at beg of next 8 rows. 15 sts.

Cast off 3 sts at beg of next 2 rows.

Cast off rem 9 sts.

Using photograph as a guide, lay elbow patches onto RS of sleeves and sew in place.

See information page for finishing instructions, setting in sleeves using the set-in method.

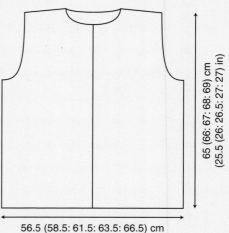

65 (66: 67: 68: 69) cm
(25.5 (26: 26.5: 27: 27) in)

56.5 (58.5: 61.5: 63.5: 66.5) cm
(22 (23: 24: 25: 26) in)

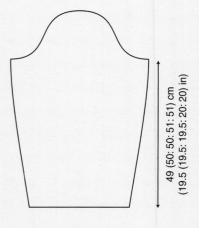

49 (50: 50: 51: 51) cm
(19.5 (19.5: 19.5: 20: 20) in)

ORIGAMI
KAFFE FASSETT

This eye-catching jumper encapsulates the rich colours of the multi-layered autumn woodland with its carpet of leaf mulch. The inspiration comes from the artists working in the first half of the 20th century – Paul Klee, Robert Delaunay and Pablo Picasso.

YARN

	S	M	L	XL	XXL	
To fit chest	97	102	107	112	117	cm
	38	40	42	44	46	in

Rowan Yorkshire Tweed 4 ply

	S	M	L	XL	XXL	
A Deep Aubergine 280						
	3	3	3	3	3	x 25gm
B Cheerful 271						
	2	2	3	3	3	x 25gm
C Bristle 278						
	2	2	2	3	3	x 25gm
D Foxy 275						
	3	3	4	4	4	x 25gm
E Radiant 276						
	2	2	2	2	3	x 25gm
F Whiskers 283						
	3	3	3	3	3	x 25gm
G Blessed 269						
	2	2	2	2	2	x 25gm
H Oceanic 285						
	2	2	2	2	2	x 25gm
J Lustre 282						
	3	3	3	3	3	x 25gm
K Sheer 267						
	1	1	1	1	2	x 25gm
L Highlander 266						
	2	2	2	2	2	x 25gm
M Enchant 268						
	1	1	1	1	1	x 25gm
N Glory 273						
	2	2	2	2	2	x 25gm
P Shrew 265						
	1	1	1	1	1	x 25gm
R Graze 286						
	2	2	2	2	2	x 25gm
S Mulled Wine 279						
	2	2	2	2	2	x 25gm
T Feral 284						
	2	2	2	2	2	x 25gm
V Knight 281						
	2	2	2	2	2	x 25gm

NEEDLES

1 pair 2³/₄ mm (no 12) (US 2) needles
1 pair 3¹/₄ mm (no 10) (US 3) needles

TENSION

26 sts and 38 rows to 10 cm measured over patterned stocking stitch using 3¹/₄ mm (US 3) needles.

BACK

Cast on 147 (153: 159: 165: 171) sts using 2³/₄ mm (US 2) needles and yarn A.
**Row 1 (RS): K1, *P1, K1, rep from * to end.
Row 2: P1, *K1, P1, rep from * to end.
These 2 rows form rib.
Joining in and breaking off colours as required, cont in rib in stripes as folls:
Using yarn B, work 2 rows.
Using yarn C, work 2 rows.
Using yarn D, work 2 rows.
Using yarn E, work 2 rows.
Using yarn A, work 2 rows.
Using yarn E, work 2 rows.
Using yarn D, work 2 rows.
Using yarn C, work 2 rows.
Using yarn B, work 2 rows.
Using yarn F, work 2 rows.**
Change to 3¹/₄mm (US 3) needles.
Starting and ending rows as indicated and using the **intarsia** technique as described on the information page, cont in patt from chart, which is worked entirely in st st beg with a K row, as folls:
Cont straight until chart row 114 (114: 118: 118: 122) has been completed, ending with a WS row. (Back should measure 35 (35: 36: 36: 37) cm.)

Shape armholes

Keeping patt correct, cast off 8 sts at beg of next 2 rows.
131 (137: 143: 149: 155) sts.
Dec 1 st at each end of next 5 rows.
121 (127: 133: 139: 145) sts.

Cont straight until chart row 208 (212: 216: 220: 224) has been completed, ending with a WS row. (Armhole should measure 25 (26: 26: 27: 27) cm.)

Shape shoulders and back neck

Cast off 12 (13: 14: 14: 15) sts at beg of next 2 rows.
97 (101: 105: 111: 115) sts.
Next row (RS): Cast off 12 (13: 14: 14: 15) sts, patt until there are 16 (16: 17: 19: 19) sts on right needle and turn, leaving rem sts on a holder.
Work each side of neck separately.
Cast off 4 sts at beg of next row.
Cast off rem 12 (12: 13: 15: 15) sts.
With RS facing, rejoin yarns to rem sts, cast off centre 41 (43: 43: 45: 47) sts, patt to end.
Complete to match first side, reversing shapings.

FRONT

Work as given for back until chart row 186 (190: 192: 196: 200) has been completed, ending with a WS row.

Shape neck

Next row (RS): Patt 51 (53: 57: 59: 61) sts and turn, leaving rem sts on a holder.
Work each side of neck separately.
Cast off 4 sts at beg of next row.
47 (49: 53: 55: 57) sts.
Dec 1 st at neck edge of next 7 rows, then on foll 3 (3: 4: 4: 4) alt rows, then on foll 4th row.
36 (38: 41: 43: 45) sts.
Work 3 rows, ending with a WS row.

Shape shoulder

Cast off 12 (13: 14: 14: 15) sts at beg of next and foll alt row.
Work 1 row.
Cast off rem 12 (12: 13: 15: 15) sts.
With RS facing, rejoin yarns to rem sts, cast off centre 19 (21: 19: 21: 23) sts, patt to end.
Complete to match first side, reversing shapings.

SLEEVES (both alike)

Cast on 73 (73: 75: 77: 77) sts using 2³/₄mm (US 2) needles and yarn A.

Work as given for back from ** to **.

Change to 3¹/₄mm (US 3) needles.

Starting and ending rows as indicated, cont in patt from chart, shaping sides by inc 1 st at each end of 7th and every foll 6th row to 103 (95: 101: 103: 103) sts, then on every foll 4th row until there are 131 (137: 137: 141: 141) sts, taking inc sts into patt.

Cont straight until chart row 164 (168: 168: 172: 172) has been completed, ending with a WS row. (Sleeve should measure 48 (49: 49: 50: 50) cm.)

Shape top

Keeping patt correct, cast off 8 sts at beg of next 2 rows.

115 (121: 121: 125: 125) sts.

Dec 1 st at each end of next and foll 5 alt rows.

Work 1 row, ending with a WS row.

Cast off rem 103 (109: 109: 113: 113) sts.

MAKING UP

PRESS as described on the information page. Join right shoulder seam using back stitch, or mattress stitch if preferred.

Neckband

With RS facing, using 2³/₄mm (US 2) needles and yarn E, pick up and knit 26 (26: 28: 28: 28) sts down left side of neck, 19 (21: 19: 21: 23) sts from front, 26 (26: 28: 28: 28) sts up right side of neck, then 50 (52: 52: 54: 56) sts from back.

121 (125: 127: 131: 135) sts.

Beg with row 2, work in rib as given for back as folls:

Using yarn E, work 1 row.

Using yarn D, work 2 rows.

Using yarn C, work 2 rows.

Using yarn B, work 2 rows.

Using yarn A, work 1 row.

Using yarn A, cast off in rib (on WS).

See information page for finishing instructions, setting in sleeves using the set-in method.

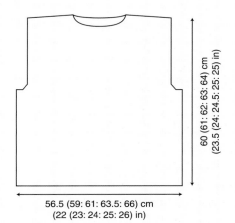

56.5 (59: 61: 63.5: 66) cm
(22 (23: 24: 25: 26) in)

60 (61: 62: 63: 64) cm
(23.5 (24: 24.5: 25: 25) in)

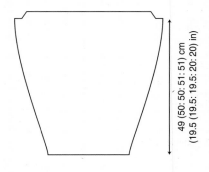

49 (50: 50: 51: 51) cm
(19.5 (19.5: 19.5: 20: 20) in)

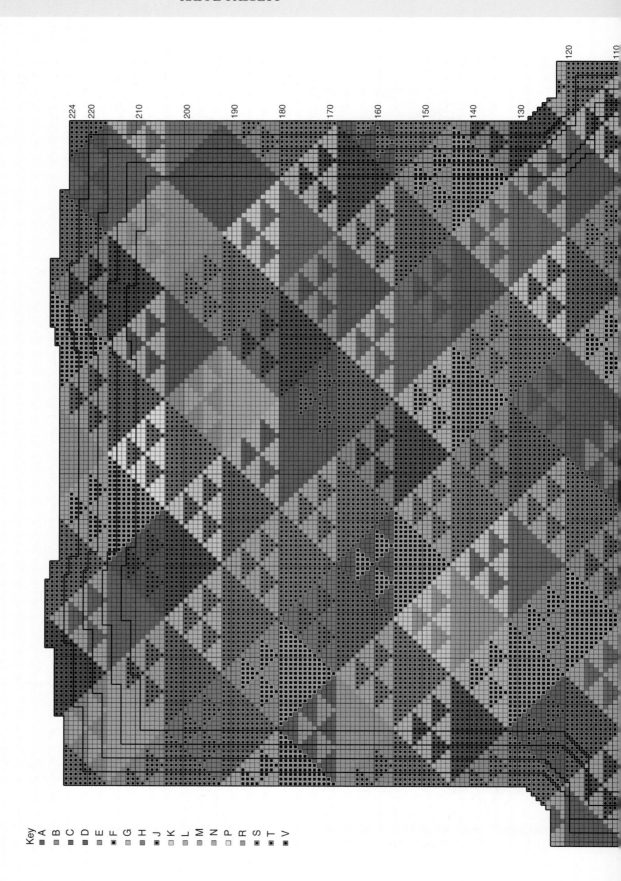

Key A B C D E F G H J K L M N P R S T V

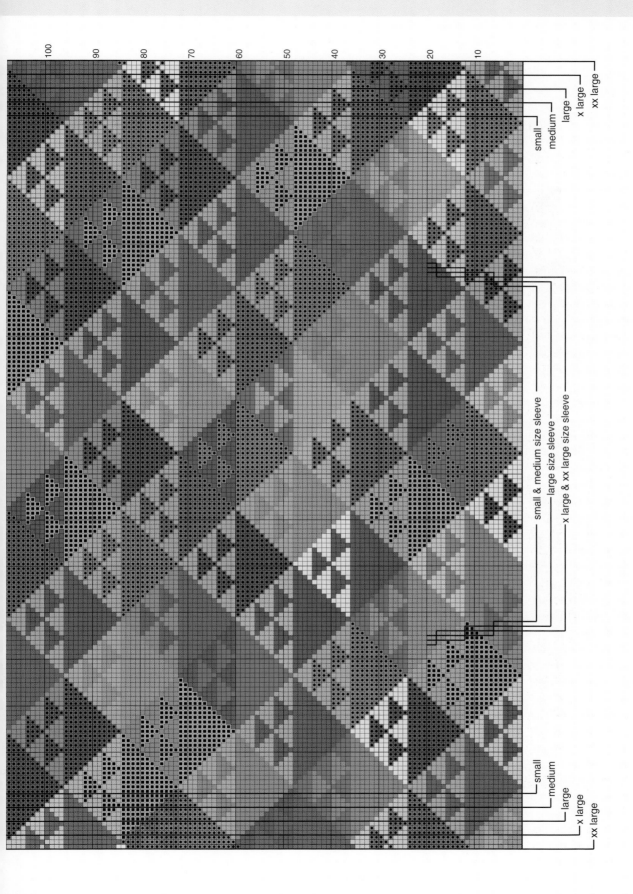

MILI

LUCINDA GUY

This little top has a film-star look, reminiscent of Audrey Hepburn in the movie Breakfast at Tiffany's. The scalloped neck, little sleeves and wavy edgings give it a real period feel. Any accessories would detract from this jewelled look: it needs no embellishment.

YARN

	XS	S	M	L	XL	
To fit bust	81	86	91	97	102	cm
	32	34	36	38	40	in

Rowan 4 ply Soft

A Wink 377						
	5	5	6	6	7	x 50gm
B Honk 374						
	1	1	1	1	1	x 50gm
C Beetroot 382						
	1	1	1	1	1	x 50gm
D Splash 373						
	1	1	1	1	1	x 50gm
E Black 383						
	1	1	1	1	1	x 50gm

NEEDLES

1 pair 2³/₄ mm (no 12) (US 2) needles
1 pair 3¹/₄ mm (no 10) (US 3) needles

CROCHET HOOK

2.00mm (no 14) (US B1) crochet hook

TENSION

28 sts and 36 rows to 10 cm measured over stocking stitch using 3¹/₄ mm (US 3) needles.

CROCHET ABBREVIATIONS

dc = double crochet; **ch** = chain;
ss = slip stitch.

BACK

Cast on 114 (121: 129: 136: 142) sts using 2³/₄ mm (US 2) needles and yarn E.
Row 1 (RS): K6 (1: 5: 0: 3), *K1, P2, K2tog tbl, (K1, yfwd) 6 times, K1, K2tog, P2, K1, rep from * to last 6 (1: 5: 0: 3) sts, K6 (1: 5: 0: 3).
138 (149: 157: 168: 174) sts.

Row 2: P6 (1: 5: 0: 3), *P1, K2, P15, K2, P1, rep from * to last 6 (1: 5: 0: 3) sts, P6 (1: 5: 0: 3).
Row 3: K6 (1: 5: 0: 3), *K1, P2, K3tog tbl, K9, K3tog, P2, K1, rep from * to last 6 (1: 5: 0: 3) sts, K6 (1: 5: 0: 3).
114 (121: 129: 136: 142) sts.
Row 4: P6 (1: 5: 0: 3), *P1, K2, P11, K2, P1, rep from * to last 6 (1: 5: 0: 3) sts, P6 (1: 5: 0: 3).
These 4 rows form patt.
Joining in and breaking off colours as required, cont in patt in stripes as folls:
Using yarn C, work 4 rows.
Using yarn B, work 4 rows.
Using yarn A, work 4 rows.
Using yarn C, work 4 rows.
Using yarn B, work 4 rows.
Using yarn A, work 4 rows.
Using yarn B, work 4 rows.
Using yarn A, work 4 rows, inc (-: -: dec: inc) 1 (-: -: 1: 1) st at end of last row.
115 (121: 129: 135: 143) sts.
Break off contrasts and cont using yarn A only.
Change to 3¹/₄ mm (US 3) needles.
Beg with a K row, work in st st for 2 rows, ending with a WS row.
Starting and ending rows as indicated and using the **intarsia** technique as described on the information page, work in patt from chart for border for 8 rows, ending with a WS row.
Break off contrasts and cont in st st using yarn A only.
Inc 1 st at each end of 11th and foll 20th row.
119 (125: 133: 139: 147) sts.
Cont straight until back measures 27 (28: 28: 29: 29) cm, ending with a WS row.

Shape armholes

Cast off 4 (5: 5: 6: 6) sts at beg of next 2 rows, then 3 sts at beg of foll 2 rows.
105 (109: 117: 121: 129) sts.
Dec 1 st at each end of next 5 (5: 7: 7: 9) rows, then on foll 1 (2: 2: 3: 3) alt rows, then on foll 4th row.
91 (93: 97: 99: 103) sts.
Cont straight until armhole measures 15 (15: 16: 16: 17) cm, ending with a WS row.
Starting and ending rows as indicated and using the **intarsia** technique as described on the information page, work in patt from chart for back neck for 12 rows, ending with a WS row.
Break off contrasts and cont in st st using yarn A only.
Work 2 rows, ending with a WS row.

Shape shoulders and back neck

Cast off 7 (7: 8: 8: 8) sts at beg of next 2 rows.
77 (79: 81: 83: 87) sts.
Next row (RS): Cast off 7 (7: 8: 8: 8) sts, K until there are 11 (11: 11: 11: 13) sts on right needle and turn, leaving rem sts on a holder.
Work each side of neck separately.
Cast off 4 sts at beg of next row.
Cast off rem 7 (7: 7: 7: 9) sts.
With RS facing, rejoin yarn to rem sts, cast off centre 41 (43: 43: 45: 45) sts, K to end.
Complete to match first side, reversing shapings.

FRONT

Work as given for back until 4 rows less have been worked than on back to beg of armhole shaping, ending with a WS row.
Next row (RS): Using yarn A K48 (51: 55: 58: 62), work next 23 sts as row 1 of chart for motif, using yarn A K to end.

MILI
LUCINDA GUY

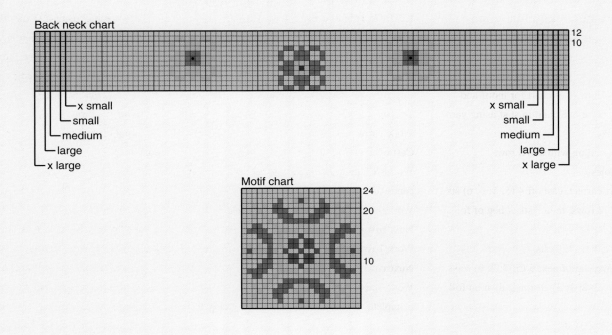

Back neck chart

12
10

x small
small
medium
large
x large

x small
small
medium
large
x large

Motif chart

24
20

10

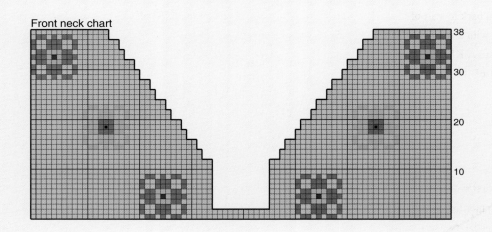

Front neck chart

38

30

20

10

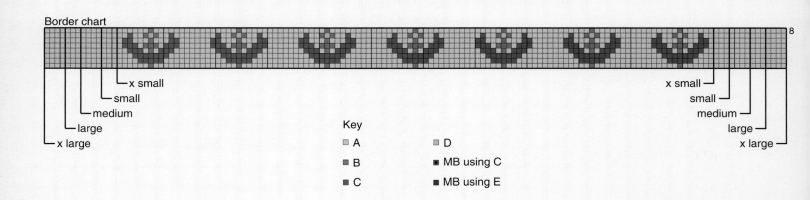

Border chart

8

x small
small
medium
large
x large

x small
small
medium
large
x large

Key

A   D

B   ■ MB using C

C   ■ MB using E

130

Next row: Using yarn A P48 (51: 55: 58: 62), work next 23 sts as row 2 of chart for motif, using yarn A P to end.

These 2 rows set the sts – centre 23 sts foll chart for motif and rem sts in st st using yarn A.

Working rem 22 rows of chart for motif and then working sts above chart in st st using yarn A, cont as folls:

Work 2 rows, ending with a WS row.

Shape armholes

Keeping chart correct, cast off 4 (5: 5: 6: 6) sts at beg of next 2 rows, then 3 sts at beg of foll 2 rows.

105 (109: 117: 121: 129) sts.

Dec 1 st at each end of next 5 (5: 7: 7: 9) rows, then on foll 1 (2: 2: 3: 3) alt rows, then on foll 4th row.

91 (93: 97: 99: 103) sts.

Cont straight until 42 (42: 42: 44: 44) rows less have been worked than on back to start of shoulder shaping, ending with a WS row.

Next row (RS): Using yarn A K5 (6: 8: 9: 11), work next 81 sts as row 1 of chart for front neck, using yarn A K to end.

Next row: Using yarn A P5 (6: 8: 9: 11), work next 81 sts as row 2 of chart for front neck, using yarn A P to end.

These 2 rows set the sts – centre 81 sts foll chart for front neck and rem sts in st st using yarn A.

Working rem 36 rows of chart for front neck and then working sts above chart in st st using yarn A, cont as folls:

Divide for neck

Next row (RS): Patt 40 (41: 43: 44: 46) sts and turn, leaving rem sts on a holder.

Work each side of neck separately.

Work 9 rows, ending with a WS row.

Next row (RS): Patt to last 5 sts, K3tog tbl, K2.

Work 1 row.

Next row: Patt to last 4 sts, K2tog tbl, K2.

Work 1 row.

Rep last 4 rows 5 (5: 5: 6: 6) times more.

22 (23: 25: 23: 25) sts.

Next row (RS): Patt to last 4 (5: 5: 0: 0) sts,

(K2tog tbl, K2) 1 (0: 0: 0: 0) times, (K3tog tbl, K2) 0 (1: 1: 0: 0) times.

21 (21: 23: 23: 25) sts.

Work 5 (5: 5: 3: 3) rows, end with a WS row.

Shape shoulder

Cast off 7 (7: 8: 8: 8) sts at beg of next and foll alt row.

Work 1 row.

Cast off rem 7 (7: 7: 7: 9) sts.

With RS facing, rejoin yarn to rem sts, cast off centre 11 sts, patt to end.

Work 9 rows, ending with a WS row.

Next row (RS): K2, K3tog, patt to end.

Work 1 row.

Next row: K2, K2tog, patt to end.

Work 1 row.

Complete to match first side, reversing shapings.

SLEEVES (both alike)

Cast on 83 (85: 89: 91: 95) sts using 3¼ mm (US 3) needles and yarn A.

Beg with a K row, work in st st for 6 rows, ending with a WS row.

Inc 1 st at each end of next and foll 6th row, then on every foll 4th row until there are 91 (93: 97: 99: 103) sts.

Work 9 rows, ending with a WS row.

Shape top

Cast off 4 (5: 5: 6: 6) sts at beg of next 2 rows, then 3 sts at beg of foll 2 rows.

77 (77: 81: 81: 85) sts.

Dec 1 st at each end of next 5 rows, then on foll 3 alt rows, then on every foll 4th row until 49 (49: 53: 53: 57) sts rem.

Work 1 row, ending with a WS row.

Dec 1 st at each end of next and every foll alt row to 37 sts, then on foll 3 rows, end with a WS row.

Cast off rem 31 sts.

MAKING UP

PRESS as described on the information page.

Join both shoulder seams using back stitch, or mattress stitch if preferred.

Neck edging

With RS facing, using 2.00mm (US B1) crochet hook and yarn A, rejoin yarn at right shoulder seam and work one round of dc evenly around entire neck edge, working 2 dc into corners and ensuring edging lays flat, ss to first dc, turn.

Breaking off and joining in colours as required, cont as folls:

Next round: Using yarn E, 1 ch (does NOT count as st), 1 dc into each dc to end, missing dc and working extra as required to ensure edging lays flat, ss to first dc, turn.

Using yarn C, rep last round once.

Using yarn B, rep last round once.

Using yarn A, rep last round once.

Fasten off.

See information page for finishing instructions, setting in sleeves using the set-in method. Work edging around cast-on edge of sleeves to match neck edging.

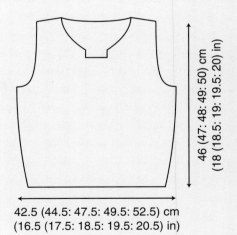

42.5 (44.5: 47.5: 49.5: 52.5) cm
(16.5 (17.5: 18.5: 19.5: 20.5) in)

46 (47: 48: 49: 50) cm
(18 (18.5: 19: 19.5: 20) in)

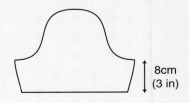

8cm
(3 in)

ALOUETTE
SARAH DALLAS

This top has a definite 50's flavour with its wavy lines and elbow length sleeves.
It is feminine and light, making the ideal match for this ballet-style layered skirt,
giving a look which is both fun and glamorous.

YARN

	XS	S	M	L	XL	
To fit bust	81	86	91	97	102	cm
	32	34	36	38	40	in

Rowan 4 ply Soft

A Irish Cream 386						
	3	3	4	4	4	x 50gm
B Day Dream 378						
	2	2	3	3	3	x 50gm
C Expresso 389						
	1	1	1	1	1	x 50gm
D Beetroot 382						
	1	1	1	1	2	x 50gm

NEEDLES

1 pair 2³/₄ mm (no 12) (US 2) needles
1 pair 3¹/₄ mm (no 10) (US 3) needles

TENSION

30 sts and 34 rows to 10 cm measured over
pattern using 3¹/₄ mm (US 3) needles.

Pattern note: In order to ensure pattern is kept
correct, place a marker on needle at beg of first
full patt rep and at end of last full patt rep.
When working sts either side of these markers,
ensure a decrease is made for every increase so
that number of sts remain correct.

BACK

Cast on 111 (117: 125: 131: 137) sts using
2³/₄ mm (US 2) needles and yarn D.
Break off yarn D and join in yarn A.
Row 1 (RS): K1, *P1, K1, rep from * to end.
Row 2: P1, *K1, P1, rep from * to end.
These 2 rows form rib.
Work in rib for 6 cm, ending with a RS row.

Next row (WS): Rib 3 (2: 6: 5: 4), M1,
*rib 4, M1, rep from * to last 4 (3: 7: 6: 5) sts,
rib to end.
138 (146: 154: 162: 170) sts.
Change to 3¹/₄ mm (US 3) needles.
Row 1 (RS): Knit.
Row 2: K3 (0: 0: 0: 1), P6 (0: 0: 3: 6), K6 (1:
5: 6: 6), *K6, P6, K6, rep from * to last 15 (1:
5: 9: 13) sts, K6 (1: 5: 6: 6), P6 (0: 0: 3: 6),
K3 (0: 0: 0: 1).
Row 3: K3 (1: 2: 3: 1), (K2tog) 1 (0: 0: 0: 1)
times, (K1, yfwd) 4 (0: 1: 2: 4) times, (K2tog)
3 (0: 1: 2: 3) times, *(K2tog) 3 times, (K1,
yfwd) 6 times, (K2tog) 3 times, rep from * to
last 15 (1: 5: 9: 13) sts, (K2tog) 3 (0: 1: 2: 3)
times, (K1, yfwd) 4 (0: 1: 2: 4) times, (K2tog)
1 (0: 0: 0: 1) times, K3 (1: 2: 3: 1).
Row 4: Purl.
These 4 rows form patt.
Keeping patt correct, cont in stripes as folls:
Using yarn C, work 2 rows.
Using yarn A, work 2 rows.
Using yarn C, work 2 rows.
Using yarn A, work 6 rows.
Using yarn B, work 8 rows.
Using yarn D, work 2 rows.
Using yarn A, work 2 rows.
Using yarn D, work 2 rows.
Using yarn B, work 8 rows.
Using yarn A, work 2 rows.
Last 40 rows form stripe sequence.
Cont in patt and stripes until back measures
28 (29: 29: 30: 30) cm, ending with a WS row.
Shape armholes
Keeping patt correct, cast off 5 (6: 6: 7: 7) sts
at beg of next 2 rows, then 4 sts at beg of
foll 2 rows. 120 (126: 134: 140: 148) sts.

Dec 1 st at each end of next 5 (5: 7: 7: 9) rows,
then on foll 1 (2: 2: 3: 3) alt rows, then on foll
4th row.
106 (110: 114: 118: 122) sts.
Cont straight until armhole measures 19 (19:
20: 20: 21) cm, ending with a WS row.
Shape back neck
Next row (RS): Patt 28 (29: 31: 32: 34) sts and
turn, leaving rem sts on a holder.
Work each side of neck separately.
Work 3 rows, ending with a WS row.
Shape shoulder
Cast off 9 (10: 10: 11: 11) sts at beg of next
and foll alt row.
Work 1 row.
Cast off rem 10 (9: 11: 10: 12) sts.
With RS facing, rejoin appropriate yarn to rem sts,
cast off centre 50 (52: 52: 54: 54) sts, patt to end.
Complete to match first side, reversing shaping.

FRONT

Work as given for back until 24 rows less have
been worked than on back to start of shoulder
shaping, ending with a WS row.
Shape front neck
Next row (RS): Patt 28 (29: 31: 32: 34) sts and
turn, leaving rem sts on a holder.
Work each side of neck separately.
Work 23 rows, ending with a WS row.
Shape shoulder
Cast off 9 (10: 10: 11: 11) sts at beg of next
and foll alt row.
Work 1 row.
Cast off rem 10 (9: 11: 10: 12) sts.
With RS facing, rejoin appropriate yarn to rem sts,
cast off centre 50 (52: 52: 54: 54) sts, patt to end.
Complete to match first side, reversing shaping.

SLEEVES (both alike)

Cast on 81 (81: 83: 85: 85) sts using 2³/₄ mm
(US 2) needles and yarn D.

Break off yarn D and join in yarn A.

Work in rib as given for back for 3 cm, ending
with a RS row.

Next row (WS): Rib 4 (5: 5: 6: 2), M1, *rib 9
(7: 6: 6: 5), M1, rep from * to last 5 (6: 6: 7: 3)
sts, rib to end.

90 (92: 96: 98: 102) sts.

Change to 3¹/₄ mm (US 3) needles.

Join in yarn B.

Row 1 (RS): Knit.

Row 2: K0 (1: 3: 4: 6), *K6, P6, K6, rep from
* to last 0 (1: 3: 4: 6) sts, K0 (1: 3: 4: 6).

Row 3: K0 (1: 3: 2: 4), (yfwd, K2tog) 0 (0: 0:
1: 1) times, *(K2tog) 3 times, (K1, yfwd) 6
times, (K2tog) 3 times, rep from * to last 0 (1:
3: 4: 6) sts, (K2tog, yfwd) 0 (0: 0: 1: 1) times,
K0 (1: 3: 2: 4).

Row 4: Purl.

These 4 rows form patt.

Working a further 4 rows using yarn B (and
then 2 rows using yarn D), cont in patt and

stripe sequence as given for back until sleeve
measures 11 cm, ending with a WS row.

Shape top

Keeping patt and stripes correct, cast off 5 (6:
6: 7: 7) sts at beg of next 2 rows, then 4 sts at
beg of foll 2 rows.

72 (72: 76: 76: 80) sts.

Dec 1 st at each end of next 5 rows, then on
foll 2 alt rows, then on every foll 4th row until
48 (48: 52: 52: 56) sts rem.

Work 1 row, ending with a WS row.

Dec 1 st at each end of next and every foll alt
row to 40 sts, then on foll 5 rows, ending with
a WS row.

30 sts.

Cast off 6 sts at beg of next 2 rows.

Cast off rem 18 sts.

MAKING UP

PRESS as described on the information page.

Join right shoulder seam using back stitch, or
mattress stitch if preferred.

Neckband

With RS facing, using 2³/₄ mm (US 2) needles

and yarn A, pick up and knit 22 (22: 22:
24: 24) sts down left side of front neck, 1 st
from corner (mark this st), 49 (51: 51:
53: 53) sts from front, 1 st from corner (mark
this st), 22 (22: 22: 24: 24) sts up right side
of front neck, 7 sts down right side of back
neck, 1 st from corner (mark this st),
49 (51: 51: 53: 53) sts from back, 1 st from
corner (mark this st), then 7 sts up left side
of back neck.

160 (164: 164: 172: 172) sts.

Row 1 (WS): *K1, P1, rep from * to end.

This row sets position of rib.

Keeping rib correct, cont as folls:

Row 2: *Rib to within 2 sts of marked st,
P2tog, K marked st, P2tog tbl, rep from * 3
times more, rib to end.

Row 3: *Rib to marked st, P marked st, rep
from * 3 times more, rib to end.

Rep last 2 rows twice more.

Cast off in rib, still decreasing either side of
marked sts as before.

See information page for finishing instructions,
setting in sleeves using the set-in method.

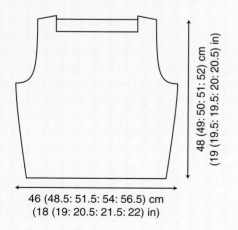

46 (48.5: 51.5: 54: 56.5) cm
(18 (19: 20.5: 21.5: 22) in)

48 (49: 50: 51: 52) cm
(19 (19.5: 19.5: 20: 20.5) in)

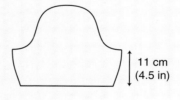

11 cm
(4.5 in)

ROWAN OVERSEAS DISTRIBUTORS

AUSTRALIA
Australian Country Spinners
314 Albert Street,
Brunswick
Victoria 3056.
Tel: (03) 9380 3888

BELGIUM
Pavan
Meerlaanstraat 73
B9860 Balegem (Oosterzele)
Tel: (32) 9 221 8594

CANADA
Diamond Yarn
9697 St Laurent,
Montreal
Quebec H3L 2N1
Tel: (514) 388 6188
www.diamondyarns.com

Diamond Yarn (Toronto)
155 Martin Ross,
Unit 3
Toronto,
Ontario M3J 2L9
Tel: (416) 736 6111
www.diamondyarns.com

DENMARK
Individual stockists -
please contact Rowan for details

FRANCE
Elle Tricote
8 Rue du Coq
67000 Strasbourg
Tel: (33) 3 88 23 03 13
www.elletricote.com

GERMANY
Wolle & Design
Wolfshovener Strasse 76
52428 Julich-Stetternich
Tel : (49) 2461 54735.
www.wolleundesign.de

HOLLAND
de Afstap
Oude Leliestraat 12
1015 AW Amsterdam
Tel : (31) 20 6231445

HONG KONG
East Unity Co Ltd
Unit B2
7/F, Block B
Kailey Industrial Centre
12 Fung Yip Street
Chai Wan
Tel : (852) 2869 7110.

ICELAND
Storkurinn
Laugavegi 59
Reykjavik
Tel: (354) 551 82 58

JAPAN
Puppy Co Ltd
TOC Building
7-22-17 Nishigotanda
Shinagwa-Ku
Tokyo
Tel : (81) 3 3494 2435

NEW ZEALAND
Individual stockists -
please contact Rowan for details

NORWAY
Paa Pinne
Tennisun 3D
0777 OSLO
Tel: (47) 909 62 818
www.paapinne.no

SWEDEN
Wincent
Norrtulsgaten 65
11345 Stockholm
Tel: (46) 8 673 70 60

U.S.A.
Rowan USA
4 Townsend West
Suite 8
Nashua
New Hampshire 03063
Tel: (1 603) 886 5041/5043

For details of U.K. stockists or any other information concerning this book please contact:

R O W A N

Rowan Yarns, Green Lane Mill, Holmfirth, West Yorkshire HD9 2DX
Tel: +44 (0)1484 681881   Fax: +44 (0)1484 687920
Email: vintagestyle@knitrowan.com   Web: www.knitrowan.com

TENSION

Obtaining the correct tension is perhaps the single factor which can make the difference between a successful garment and a disastrous one. It controls both the shape and size of an article, so any variation, however slight, can distort the finished garment.

Different designers feature in our books and it is **their** tension, given at the **start** of each pattern, which you must match. We recommend that you knit a square in pattern and/or stocking stitch (depending on the pattern instructions) of perhaps 5 - 10 more stitches and 5 - 10 more rows than those given in the tension note. Press the finished square under a damp cloth and mark out the central 10cm square with pins. If you have too many stitches to 10cm try again using thicker needles, if you have too few stitches to 10cm try again using finer needles. Once you have achieved the correct tension your garment will be knitted to the measurements indicated in the size diagram shown at the end of the pattern.

SIZING AND SIZE DIAGRAM NOTE

The instructions are given for the smallest size. Where they vary, work the figures in brackets for the larger sizes. **One set of figures refers to all sizes.** Included with every pattern in this magazine is a '**size diagram**', or sketch of the finished garment and its dimensions. The purpose of this is to enable you to accurately achieve a perfect fitting garment without the need for worry during knitting. The size diagram shows the finished width of the garment at the under-arm point, and it is this measurement that the knitter should choose first; a useful tip is to measure one of your own garments which is a comfortable fit. Having chosen a size based on width, look at the corresponding length for that size; if you are not happy with the total length which we recommend, adjust your own garment before beginning your armhole shaping - any adjustment after this point will mean that your sleeve will not fit into your garment easily - don't forget to take your adjustment into account if there is any side seam shaping. Finally, look at the sleeve length; the size diagram shows the finished sleeve measurement, taking into account any top-arm insertion length. Measure your body between the centre of your neck and your wrist, this measurement should correspond to half the garment width plus the sleeve length. Again, your sleeve length may be adjusted, but remember to take into consideration your sleeve increases if you do adjust the length - you must increase more frequently than the pattern states to shorten your sleeve, less frequently to lengthen it.

CHART NOTE

Many of the patterns in the book are worked from charts. Each square on a chart represents a stitch and each line of squares a row of knitting. Each colour used is given a different symbol or letter and these are shown in the **materials** section, or in the

key alongside the chart of each pattern.
When working from the charts, read odd rows (K) from right to left and even rows (P) from left to right, unless otherwise stated.

KNITTING WITH COLOUR

There are two main methods of working colour into a knitted fabric: **Intarsia** and **Fairisle** techniques. The first method produces a single thickness of fabric and is usually used where a colour is only required in a particular area of a row and does not form a repeating pattern across the row, as in the fairisle technique.

Intarsia: The simplest way to do this is to cut short lengths of yarn for each motif or block of colour used in a row. Then joining in the various colours at the appropriate point on the row, link one colour to the next by twisting them around each other where they meet on the wrong side to avoid gaps. All ends can then either be darned along the colour join lines, as each motif is completed or then can be 'knitted-in' to the fabric of the knitting as each colour is worked into the pattern. This is done in much the same way as 'weaving-in' yarns when working the Fairisle technique and does save time darning-in ends. It is essential that the tension is noted for **Intarsia** as this may vary from the stocking stitch if both are used in the same pattern.

Fairisle type knitting: When two or three colours are worked repeatedly across a row, strand the yarn **not** in use loosely behind the stitches being worked. If you are working with more than two colours, treat the 'floating' yarns as if they were one yarn and always spread the stitches to their correct width to keep them elastic. It is advisable not to carry the stranded or 'floating' yarns over more than three stitches at a time, but to weave them under and over the colour you are working. The 'floating' yarns are therefore caught at the back of the work.

ALL ribs should be knitted to a firm tension, for some knitters it may be necessary to use a smaller needle. In order to prevent sagging in cuffs and welts we suggest you use a 'knitting-in' elastic.

CROCHET TERMS

UK crochet terms and abbreviations have been used throughout. The list below gives the US equivalent where they vary.

Abbreviation	UK	US
dc	double crochet	single crochet
htr	half treble	half treble crochet
tr	treble	double crochet
dtr	double treble	treble
ttr	triple treble	double treble
qtr	quadruple treble	triple treble

SLIP STITCH EDGINGS

When a row end edge forms the actual finished edge of a garment, you will often find a slip stitch edging is worked along this edge.
To work a slip stitch edging at the end of a RS

row, work across the row until there is one st left on the left needle. Pick up the loop lying between the needles and place this loop on the right needle. Please note that this loop does NOT count as a st and is not included in any st counts. Now slip the last stitch knitwise with the yarn at the back (WS) of the work. At the beginning of the next row P together the first (slipped) stitch with the picked-up loop.

To work a slip stitch edging at the end of a WS row, work across the row until there is one st left on the left needle. Pick up the loop lying between the needles and place this loop on the right needle. Please note that this loop does NOT count as a st and is not included in any st counts. Now slip the last stitch purlwise with the yarn at the front (WS) of the work. At the beginning of the next row K together tbl the first (slipped) stitch with the picked-up loop.

FINISHING INSTRUCTIONS

After working for hours knitting a garment, it seems a great pity that many garments are spoiled because such little care is taken in the pressing and finishing process. Follow the following tips for a truly professional-looking garment.

PRESSING

Darn in all ends neatly along the selvage edge or a colour join, as appropriate.
Block out each piece of knitting using pins and gently press each piece, omitting the ribs, using a warm iron over a damp cloth. **Tip**: Take special care to press the edges, as this will make sewing up both easier and neater.

STITCHING

When stitching the pieces together, remember to match areas of colour and texture very carefully where they meet. Use a seam stitch such as back stitch or mattress stitch for all main knitting seams and join all ribs and neckband with a flat seam, unless otherwise stated.

CONSTRUCTION

Having completed the pattern instructions, join left shoulder and neckband seams as detailed above. Sew the top of the sleeve to the body of the garment using the method detailed in the pattern, referring to the appropriate guide:
Straight cast-off sleeves: Place centre of cast-off edge of sleeve to shoulder seam. Sew top of sleeve to body, using markers as guidelines where applicable.
Square set-in sleeves: Set sleeve head into armhole, the straight sides at top of sleeve to form a neat right-angle to cast-off sts at armhole on back and front.
Shallow set-in sleeves: Join cast-off sts at beg of armhole shaping to cast-off sts at start of sleeve-head shaping. Sew sleeve head into armhole, easing in shapings.
Set-in sleeves: Set in sleeve, easing sleeve head into armhole.

Join side and sleeve seams.
Slip stitch pocket edgings and linings into place.
Sew on buttons to correspond with buttonholes.
After sewing up, press seams and hems.
Ribbed welts and neckbands and any areas of garter stitch should not be pressed.

● = Easy, straight forward knitting

●● = Suitable for the average knitter

●●● = For the more experienced knitter

ABBREVIATIONS

K	knit
P	purl
st(s)	stitch(es)
inc	increas(e)(ing)
dec	decreas(e)(ing)
st st	stocking stitch (1 row K, 1 row P)
garter st	garter stitch (K every row)
beg	begin(ning)
foll	following
rem	remain(ing)
rev	revers(e)(ing)
rep	repeat
alt	alternate
cont	continue
patt	pattern
tog	together
mm	millimetres
cm	centimetres
in(s)	inch(es)
RS	right side
WS	wrong side
sl 1	slip one stitch
psso	pass slipped stitch over
p2sso	pass 2 slipped stitches over
tbl	through back of loop
M1	make one stitch by picking up horizontal loop before next stitch and knitting into back of it
M1P	make one stitch by picking up horizontal loop before next stitch and purling into back of it
yfwd	yarn forward
yon	yarn over needle
cn	cable needle